contents

dedication

To all teachers, past and present, without whom this book would not have been possible.

How to write what you want to say ... about visual images

a guide for those who know
what they want to say
but can't find the words

Patricia Hipwell, Lyn Carter and
Georgina Barton

First published 2017

National Library of Australia Cataloguing-in-Publication entry
Creator: Hipwell, Patricia, author.
Title: How to write what you want to say ... about visual images: a guide for those who know what they want to say but can't find the words/Patricia Hipwell, Lyn Carter and Georgina Barton.
ISBN: 9781925522501 (paperback), 9781925522570 (ebook)
Subjects: Creative writing.
Authorship.
Writing–Technique.
English language–Writing.
Other Creators/Contributors:
Carter, Lyn, author.
Barton, Georgina, author.

Typeset in Delicious 10 pt.

Text and cover design: **Boolarong Press**

Image of *Pencil-pusher* by Zsuzsanna Kilian

Cover images: Photograph – Man on ledge: iStock.com/Alija (stock illustration ID: 528920316) and SE Queensland rail network: reproduced with permission from Queensland Rail

Note: Text examples of the writing skill have been created to demonstrate that skill. Possible inaccuracies and out-of-date information in these texts are acknowledged by the authors and do not detract from the validity of their inclusion.

Published by Boolarong Press, Salisbury, Brisbane, Australia.

introduction

This guide, written by Patricia Hipwell, Dr Lyn Carter and Associate Professor Georgina Barton, provides students with the language they need to write about a variety of visual images. In this book, a *visual image* is a print or electronic picture or representation of something or someone, across a broad range from graphs and diagrams that present information through to artwork and photographs intended to appeal to emotions. The book aims to provide inexperienced writers with a starting point to say what they want to say about any type of visual image using language that mature writers use.

The book deals with eight common forms of writing about visual images, with six pages devoted to each form:

- The first page describes the form, or skill, of the writing, gives some tips for students and provides a graphic organiser that can be used to support students as they plan that form of writing about a visual image.
- The second page provides examples of sentence starters commonly used in that skill.
- The third through to sixth pages give four examples of the skill when writing about different types of visual images.

Additional sections at the end of the book provide more general information to improve the sophistication of the writing.

How to write what you want to say ... about visual images is a guide for those who know what they want to say but can't find the words. It provides a unique tool for improving writing about visual images. It suits inexperienced writers from the middle years of schooling to the tertiary level.

This book is the seventh in the series and takes a similar approach to:

- *How to write what you want to say ...* by Patricia Hipwell
- *How to write what you want to say ... in mathematics* by Lyn Carter and Patricia Hipwell
- *How to write what you want to say ... in the primary years* by Catherine Black and Patricia Hipwell
- *How to write what you want to say ... in science* by Malcolm Carter, Lyn Carter and Patricia Hipwell
- *How to write what you want to say ... in business* by Lyn Carter and Patricia Hipwell
- *How to write what you want to say ... at university* by Patricia Hipwell and Lyn Carter

about visual images

Visual representations are a feature of modern life. In this book, print or electronic pictures or representations of something or someone are called *visual images*. The purpose and nature of a visual image affects the way that we write about it. In planning this book, the authors have classified visual images into two broad groups.

- **Informative:** These are the visual images used to show factual information. They include graphs of all types, number lines and Cartesian planes, timelines, musical scores, all types of maps, plans and blueprints, scale drawings, geometric diagrams, Venn diagrams, flowcharts, tree diagrams, hierarchies, networks, family trees, and icons. Visual images in this category can be further divided into those that depend on a scale (for example, most graphs and maps) and unscaled images where length or size are less important.
- **Narrative:** Visual images are used in many situations to add interest, tell a story, evoke feelings and represent attitudes. Examples include artworks, illustrations, animations, sketches, photographs, and logos. Visual images of this type are described in this book as narrative images.

The purpose and properties of visual images determine what and how we write about them. For this reason, each of the skills presented in this book is demonstrated using four different types of visual images: two informative and two narrative.

key terms and ideas defined

form of writing	the particular way of writing about a visual image, for example, describing, explaining, analysing.
purpose	the use or reason for a form of writing about a visual image, or for the visual image itself.
things to know	important information about the form of writing.
sentence starters	the opening clause of the sentence; these sentence starters are shown in bold in the examples of each form of writing; in the sentence starters the words *visual image* could be replaced with a more accurate description of the object, such as *diagram, graph, photograph, sculpture.*
graphic organiser	a tool that assists writers to organise their ideas and plan their writing.
useful language	some suggested vocabulary that is characteristic of, or commonly used in, writing about visual images (see pages 54 to 57).
connectives	words or phrases that link or connect ideas within sentences or ideas from one sentence to the next (see page 57).

critical literacy: implementing the four-resources (roles) model

what is a text?

While many think a *text* is words printed on a page, in its broadest sense *text* refers to any way in which meaning is created or made. It includes the written word, the spoken word, visual images (still and moving) and even body language. That is the way we use the word in this book. When we want to refer to the words printed on a page, we call it the *written text*.

Literacy is a complex process. When we read text, besides making a literal meaning, we need to make inferences about the deeper meaning or underlying messages of the text and analyse it critically.

Luke and Freebody (1991) developed a model that we can use to comprehend a text. Known as the Four Resources Model, it enables the readers to ask various questions to assist with interpreting a text. We, as the readers, assume the roles of code breaker, text participant, text user and text analyst.

code breaker

When we act as code breakers, we *crack the code* by recognising the codes and conventions in texts: elements such as layout including images, icons and symbols; the relationships between these aspects; and how both the text and visual image have an impact on our perspectives. All are significant for code breakers.

text participant or meaning maker

As text participants we ask the question, *What does this text mean to me?* We use our prior knowledge and experiences to make meaning of the text. Our own interests and view of the world will also influence the meaning we make from the text.

text user

As text users we ask, *What do I do with this text?* We begin to understand more about the purpose of the text and can interpret it in different contexts. Text users understand that visual images are shaped by their structure, tone and sequence.

text analyst

When we act as a text analyst, we understand that texts are not neutral. They represent particular viewpoints. We know that texts are influenced by the writer's worldview and may represent that view.

the relationship of the visual image to written texts

Some visual images are presented with words, for example, graphs in a report, diagrams in an explanation. Asking questions of the visual image enables the reader to decide if there is a relationship between the written words and the visual image and the nature of that relationship.

Questions to ask include:

a) Is the visual image vital to my interpretation of the written text (for example, the information in the visual image is not provided in the writing)?

b) Is the visual image useful, but can I obtain the information in other ways (for example, if the information is also provided in the writing)?

c) Is the visual image irrelevant to my interpretation of the written text (for example, I would not lose any information if the visual image were left out)?

d) Is the visual image outwardly confusing/misleading/contradictory (for example, it does not match the information given in the writing)?

student prompts to guide the interpretation of visual images

role/resource	informative (scaled and unscaled)	narrative
code breaker	• What type of visual image is this? • What is the purpose of the visual image? • Who is the audience for the visual image? • Where might you see this visual image? • Is there a scale? If so, what is the scale and how is it shown? • Is there a location or indication of place? • If the visual image is a map, where is north? • Is the position shown by a grid (coordinates or latitude and longitude) or by distance or angle? • Are there any abbreviations? If so, what do they stand for? • Is information conveyed by line thickness, colour saturation, colour hue, texture, icons, symbols and illustrations? • Where do I start and finish reading the visual image? • Does it matter where I start and finish reading the visual image? • Does directionality matter (i.e. top to bottom, left to right, bottom to top, etc.)? • Which typographical conventions are familiar and which are new?	• What type of visual image is this? • What is the purpose of the visual image? • Who is the audience for the visual image? • Where might you see this visual image? • What are the features of this visual image? • Can I crack the codes and conventions of this visual image? • What is the layout of this visual image? • Can I predict what the visual image will reveal? • Are there any symbols or icons used? What do they represent? • Is information conveyed by line thickness, colour saturation, colour hue, and texture? • What artistic/aesthetic elements (e.g. line, form, colour, shape) have been used in this visual image?
text participant or meaning maker	• Can I interpret the scale? • How will I read the visual image (skim, scan, closely or continuously)? • Is there a heading/title and what can I predict from this heading? • Would the shape be as meaningful if presented from another projection? • Is this visual image similar to one I have seen before? • Is it helpful to *zoom out* from the visual image to get an overall impression and then *zoom in* to focus on details? • What is the relationship between the various parts of the visual image? • If the visual image is presented with writing, then what is the function/role of the visual image?	• How will I read the visual image (skim, scan, closely or continuously)? • Is there a heading/title and what can I predict from this heading? • What is familiar about this visual image and what is unfamiliar? • What elements of design have been used to influence the viewer? • If the visual image is presented with writing, then what is the function/role of the visual image? • How would people different from me (age, gender, sexuality, race, class, 'tech savvy' or 'non-tech savvy') read the visual image? • How does this visual image function in different social and cultural contexts? • Does the visual image evoke a response from me and/or encourage me to do something? • Does this visual image evoke a response from me sufficient for me to do something with other people? • What does the visual image have to say about gender?

student prompts to guide the interpretation of visual images

text user	• Would the shape be as meaningful if presented from another projection? • Is the scale misleading (scaled)? • Is the visual image more or less complex than the information it presents? • Is this a good example of this type of visual image? • Is the visual image easy or difficult to read?	• What personal experiences do I have with the content of the visual image that help me make sense of it? • What kinds of visual images are connected with this one? • What are all the possible meanings that this visual image is trying to convey? • How does this visual image make me feel? • Is this visual image effective in conveying a message or messages? • How could another visual image on the same topic be similar or different? • How might I change the visual image to reflect my point of view or ideas about the way the world/topic should be understood or interpreted? • How does the design of the visual image contribute to its meaning?
text analyst	• How do I know if the information presented in this visual image is true or valuable? • Is there anything we should know about the visual image that is not said? • What is missing? • What does the creator of the visual image want me to believe about the topic or subject? • What would another visual image about the same topic look like if it were designed by someone else? • Does the visual image reflect my point of view about the way this topic should be interpreted? If not, how would I change it?	• Do I know who created this visual image and their reasons for doing so? • What is missing? • What is the visual image telling the viewer about what is ‘normal’ in everyday life? • Who are the ‘insiders’ and ‘outsiders’ in this visual image? • What does the visual image want me to believe? Do I agree with the way the creator of the visual image is trying to make me feel? • What meaning is the viewer invited to make from the visual image and what reading could they make? • How would a different projection change the meaning the viewer makes from the visual image?

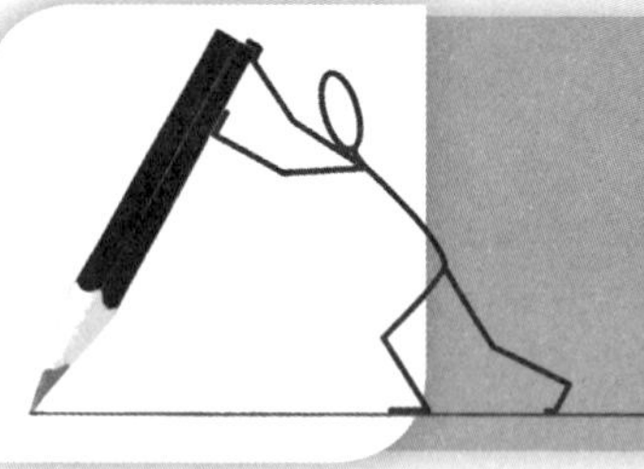

describing

meaning

giving a detailed account of the properties/qualities/features/parts of the visual image

things to know

A description should be about the features observed in the visual image. It does not interpret the meaning of those features (see the skill of interpreting *on pages 24 to 29).*

A very detailed description should allow the reader to reproduce the visual image without having seen the original. However, for most purposes, this level of detail is not required. Therefore, descriptions usually focus on the important features.

A text about a visual image will often start with a description, and then include other forms of writing.

graphic organiser for describing

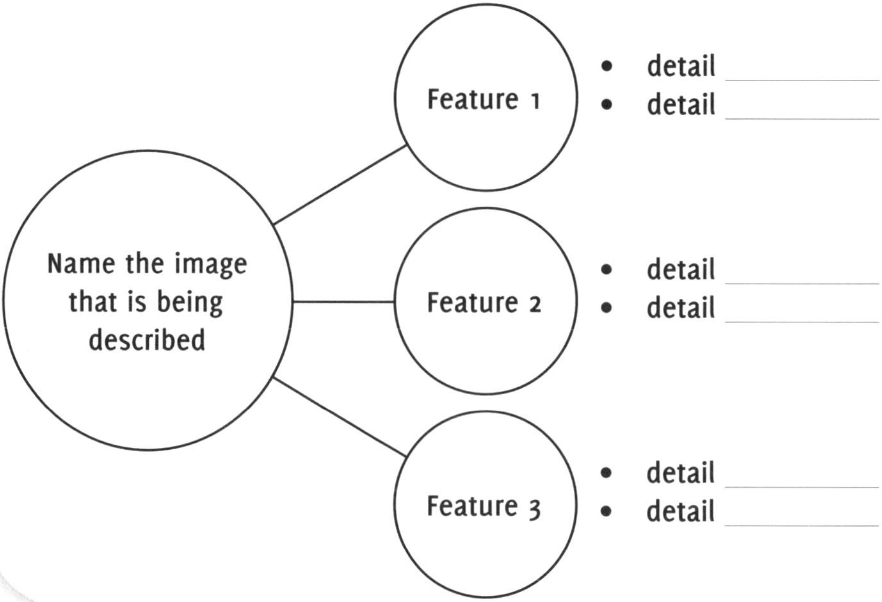

Name the image that is being described

Feature 1
- detail ____________
- detail ____________

Feature 2
- detail ____________
- detail ____________

Feature 3
- detail ____________
- detail ____________

sentence starters

This is a ... (visual image) of a/an ...
The ... (visual image) shows the (feature/s) of a ...
There are also ..., showing/which show ...
There are several ... and these ...
The ... (visual image) is similar to ... in that it is/has/is made of ...
The ... (visual image) is similar to ..., except that ...
... is/are usually made of ...
It is tempting to think that ...
The/A/An ... is depicted in this ... (visual image).
The important/key/significant features are ...
Other less significant features include ...
For clarity and simplicity, the ... (visual image) is presented in ...
The main features of this ... (visual image) are related to ...
There are a few/some/several/many ... in the ... (visual image).
This representation of ... shows ...
As a result, ...
One of the characteristics of the ... (visual image) is that ...
Another interesting feature in this ... (visual image) is ...
The ... (visual image) has several notable features, including ...
The ... (visual image) includes/is composed of/consists of/is constructed with ...
The ... (visual image) is enhanced by ...
The ... (visual image) has some distinctive features, especially ...
The most obvious/important feature of the ... (visual image) is ...
The ... (feature/s) in the (foreground/background) frame/s the ... (visual image)
... lead/s the viewer's eye to ...

example 1

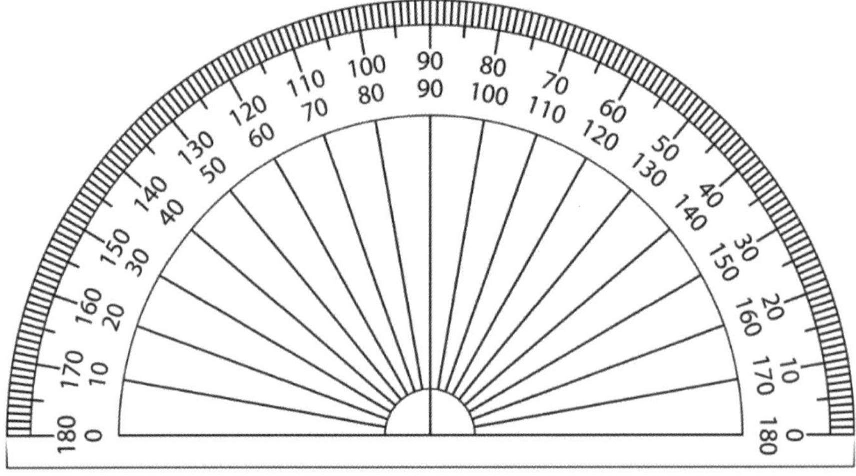

This is a diagram of a protractor. Protractors are used to measure angles, usually in degrees. This protractor is semi-circular (other protractors can be full circles or even squares). It has a scale comprising 181 equally spaced marks on the circumference, representing whole degrees. **There are also** 19 equally spaced lines on the inside of the semi-circle, **showing** angles that are multiples of 10 degrees. The two sets of numbers indicate the values of the scale. The outermost set of numbers starts with 0 on the right and proceeds in an anticlockwise direction in groups of 10 until 180 is reached on the left side. The inner set of numbers starts with 0 on the left and proceeds in a clockwise direction in groups of 10 to 180 on the right. The horizontal line labelled 0 and 180 is the base line of the protractor.

The protractor is similar to a number line or ruler, **except that** the scale is curved rather than straight. The skills used to interpret a number line can be applied to the interpretation of the protractor. However, unlike rulers, protractors use scale to measure angle size, not length. The size of protractors can vary, depending on their use.

Protractors **are usually made of** transparent plastic. This diagram of a protractor is printed in black ink on a white page, with the white paper substituting for transparent plastic.

example 2

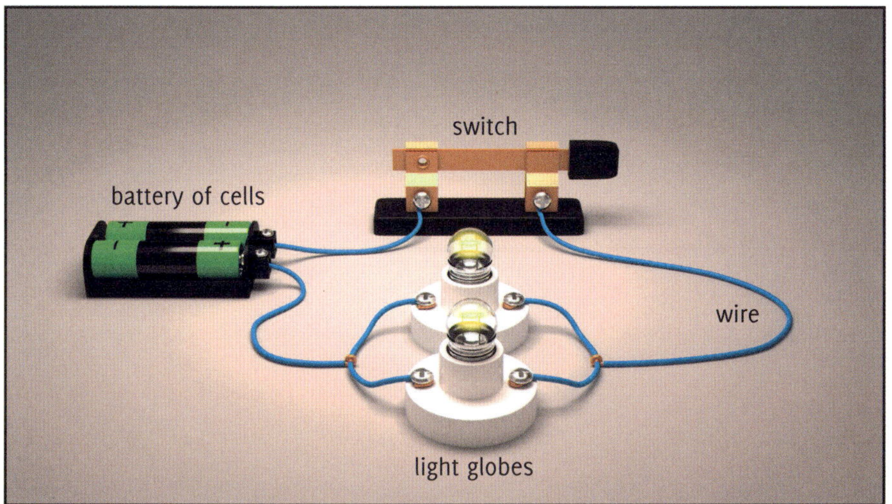

A simple electrical circuit **is depicted in this photograph. The important features are** labelled. Several components form part of this circuit. They include a battery of two cells, a switch and two light globes or lamps, all connected by wires. The paragraphs that follow describe each of these components.

The wires are coated in blue plastic, so it is not possible to see from the photograph what they are made of. Electrical wiring is usually metal, often copper. In more complicated electrical circuits with many wires, the plastic can be colour coded to make it easy to see how the wires in the circuit are connected.

The power in this circuit is provided by a battery of two cells, painted green, in a holder. Cells such as these are powered by the energy produced by a chemical reaction that takes place inside the cell. The battery holder has two terminals to which the wires are connected. In larger circuits, the energy source might differ, for example, generators, solar panels, or wind turbines.

The circuit **includes** two light globes. They are wired in parallel, so that the electrical current can pass through each globe simultaneously. In a parallel circuit, if one of the light globes is faulty so that the current can no longer pass through it, the current can continue to flow through the other part of the circuit so that the other lamp will operate.

The third component in this circuit is a switch that allows the lamps to be turned on and off. In the photograph, the lever is down so the switch is in the on position. **As a result**, the circuit is closed, the current flows, and the light globes are lit. When turned off, by moving the lever up, the electrical circuit is broken so that the current does not flow through the circuit and the lamps are not lit. The light switches found on the wall in buildings operate in the same way as the simple switch shown in this photograph.

example 3

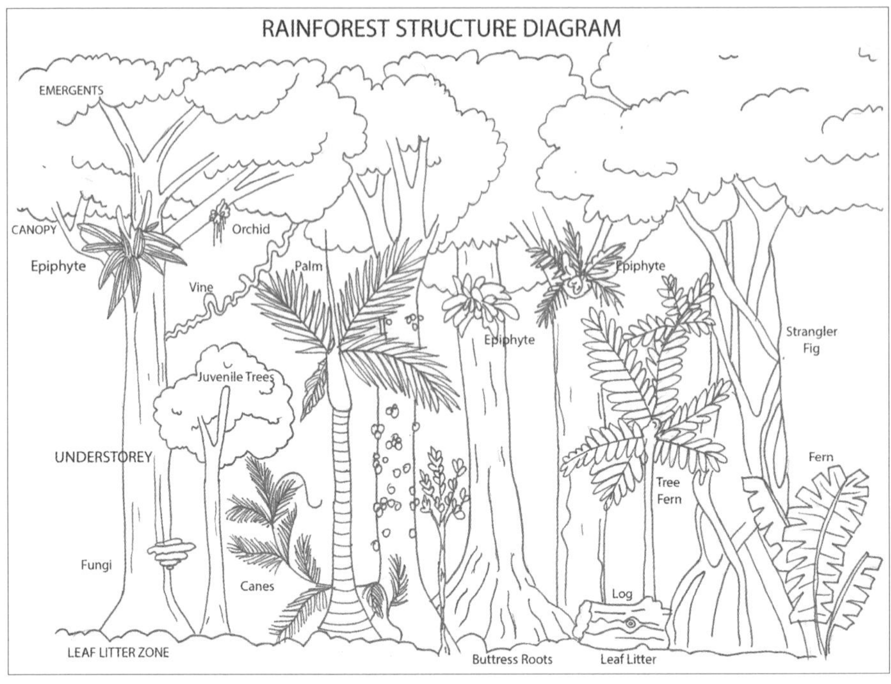

The sketch **shows the** structure **of a** tropical rainforest. Tropical rainforests are found between the Tropics of Cancer and Capricorn in areas that experience hot and wet conditions. **There are several** layers or storeys in a tropical rainforest **and these** make it distinctive. The tall trees or *emergents* grow to great heights as they struggle for sunlight. Their crowns coalesce or merge to form the canopy, which is a dense layer of vegetation that blocks out much of the sunlight to the layers below.

As a result, the plants underneath the canopy are adapted to surviving without much sunlight. Palms, canes, tree ferns and juvenile trees form the understorey and they do not grow as tall as the canopy. **An interesting feature of the rainforest** is that some types of vegetation cannot grow tall enough to reach the sunlight, so they use other vegetation as support. Epiphytes, vines and orchids grow on other plants but get their food and water from the air. Parasites, such as the Strangler Fig, use other plants for support (mostly trees) and take food and water from the host plant, eventually killing or *strangling* it.

The leaf-litter zone, at ground level, **is made up** of the leaves and branches that have fallen from above. Plants that grow here need to be able to do so with hardly any sunlight. Various forms of fungi that live on decomposing vegetation are found in this storey. With all this leaf litter, **it is tempting to think that** soil in rainforests is rich; however, it is poor quality and low in nutrients. The trees have buttress roots that do not go deeply into the soil. They spread out to keep the tree stable and also to take up the nutrients from the leaf litter.

example 4

This photographic image **features** a row of colourful houses along a cobbled street. The bright colour, front door, two windows and tiled terracotta roof of each house make it easily identifiable. The colours are predominantly primary colours of red, yellow and blue. **There are** seven smaller houses down the left-hand side of the street followed by a two-storey yellow house with burnt sienna stripes. The houses on the right-hand side are white.

The houses **in the foreground** on the left-hand side of the street **frame the** photograph. They lead towards a cream double-storey house at the end of the street. The angle of the camera achieves this perspective. Furthermore, the bright red and pink flowers in the foreground **lead the viewer's eye to** the end of the street.

Another interesting feature in this photograph **is** the two lines of different-coloured cobblestones on the right-hand side. They lead straight to the end of the street, guiding the viewer's eye and also representing salience in the visual image. The layout of houses could indicate the photograph has been taken in a country that has colder weather because the houses are close together and have chimneys.

explaining

meaning

making an idea or situation clear by showing what it is (description), how it works (process) and why it works or occurs (reasons)

things to know

When planning an explanation, it can be helpful to sort ideas into three categories: what, how *and* why. *These categories can be used as sub-headings and form the basis of the descriptions, processes and justifications included in the explanation. However, sophisticated writers might interweave the three parts. Both ways are shown in the examples.*

graphic organiser for explaining

WHAT IS BEING EXPLAINED (DESCRIPTION)?	HOW IS IT OCCURRING?	WHY IS IT OCCURRING?

sentence starters

... is a detailed representation of ...
... is/are used to show ...
... indicate ...
... are made for particular purposes, including, ...
For that reason, ... do not give much ...
The impact of ... increased from ... to ...
The changes also show/reflect ...
... also includes ...
... which represent/s the ...
... (visual images) such as this one show ...
There is a sequence behind the ...
It is difficult to know/decide which part of the ... (visual image) to view first.
... (visual image) is a detailed representation of ...
... because it is important that ...
The main effect of the use of ... is ...
The main reason that ... occurs is ...
... has made clear choices about ...
... works by ...
This happens/occurs because ...
... is also a colour that means ...
The changes also reflect ...
... has resulted in ...
The point of this is ...
A similar outcome results from ...
Also shown in the ... (visual image) is/are ...
... (visual image) depicts ...

example 1

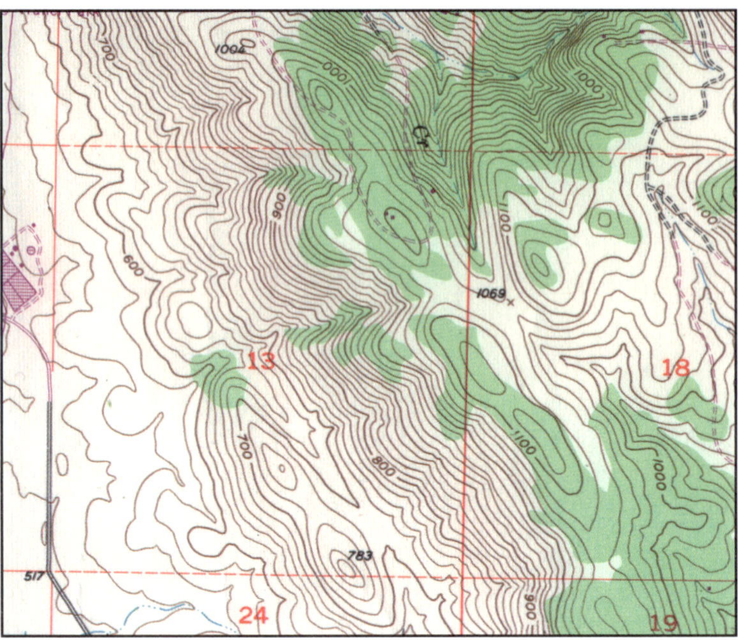

NB: The key is not included

A topographic map **is a detailed representation of** an area of land. It uses lines, shading, colour and labels to show natural landforms such as hills and mountains, rivers and streams, lakes and coastlines, and some man-made objects. North is at the top of the map, and lines of latitude and longitude are also shown. Topographic maps are drawn to scale, using a large scale to show detailed information.

A key **is used to show** the scale and meaning of symbols, lines, and shading and to give other information. Green shading shows elevation. Blue lines mark rivers or streams and blue shading denotes water bodies such as seas and lakes. Black and pink are used to indicate structures made by people such as roads and some buildings. This map shows the borders of the various sections of land, marked and numbered in red (on this map 13, 18, 24 and 19). Brown contour lines **are used to show** places of equal height above sea level (elevation). They include numbers in brown that show the elevation of that contour. In this map, the contour interval is 20, meaning that each contour line is 20 metres higher or lower than the next. Most contour lines are thin, but thicker lines are used to show the contours for heights that are multiples of 100. **The point of this is** to make it easier to interpret the elevation. Contours that are close together **indicate** steep land. Concentric circles indicate peaks, usually with a label giving the height of the summit and sometimes the name. Kinks in contours show ridges and valleys, with valleys often containing a watercourse.

Topographic maps **are made for particular purposes**, being used by hikers, the military, civil engineers and others who need to know how high and rugged the land is and about the location of landforms. **For that reason**, they **do not give much** detail about built structures such as property boundaries or cities.

example 2

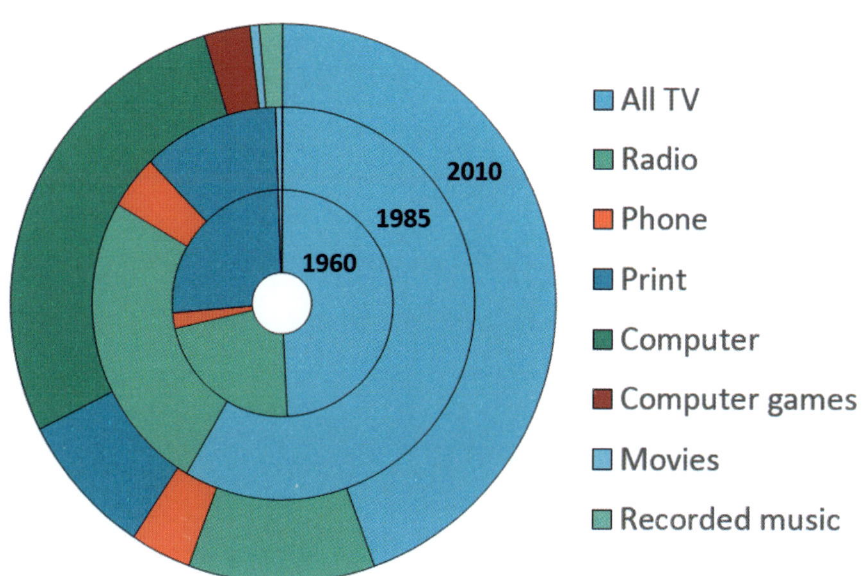

This chart shows the changes in the various ways that students have been exposed to words over the 50 years between 1960 and 2010. Three superimposed pie charts represent data at 25 year intervals: 1960, 1985 and 2010. The eight ways that students see or hear words are shown using colour. A key explains the meaning of these colours.

The pale blue sections of the chart **show that** television has always been the most significant way that students are exposed to words. Radio, shown in pale green, and print materials, shown in dark blue, are also important ways that students encounter vocabulary. In 2010 computers and computer games (dark green and dark red, respectively) have emerged as important ways that students encounter words.

Changes in students' exposure to words reflect changes in technology since 1960. **The impact of** television **increased from** 1960 to 1985, but has recently fallen as computers have become more popular. **The changes also reflect** the increasing use of telephones by young people. **This has occurred because** telephones have changed from large handsets attached to a fixed landline shared by the entire household to small, portable, wireless devices carried by most individuals.

A decline in the popularity of radio since 1960 **has resulted in a** steady reduction in the importance of radio in introducing students to new words. **A similar outcome results from** a reduction in the use of printed materials such as books.

example 3

what

This photograph **depicts** two objects – a full glass of sugar cubes on the left and a can of Coca-Cola on the right. They are side by side on wooden boards, running from the front to the back of the image, and the background is pale blue and striped. The designer of the photograph **has made clear choices** about the placement of the glass of sugar and Coca-Cola can so that the viewer can see a relationship between the two objects.

how

Both objects in the photograph are presented at eye level **because it is important that** the viewer can see the relationship and compare the objects. **The main effect of the use of** contrasting colours (the red can with the blue background) is to make the image of the can stand out. Red **is also a colour that means** dominance and power – a colour trademarked by the multinational Coca-Cola Company. The level of the sugar cubes, almost in line with the top of the can, also **has an impact** on the viewer. The designer of the photograph invites the viewer to conclude that a can of Coca-Cola contains a large amount of sugar.

why

The main reason for showing the full glass of sugar cubes next to the can of Coca-Cola **is** to highlight the large amount of sugar in a can of this soft drink. This is to inform consumers about what they are drinking and prompt them to consider healthier alternatives.

example 4

***My Mother's Country* by Robert Barton**

This acrylic painting, by the artist Robert Barton, is titled *My Mother's Country.* The painting uses colours within the same palette, that is, browns and ochres. **These** colours **are most likely to** occur in the part of Australia where the artist's mother is from – Central Queensland.

The painting **also includes** a number of iconic symbols that relate to Australian Aboriginal art, culture and community. These include the footprints of animals such as the emu, dingo and kangaroo. **Also shown in this** artwork are the sun, a star, and women sitting around campfires. For example, the women are shown as white U shapes sitting around concentric circles, which are campfires.

There is a sequence behind the creation of this artwork known as the process of layering. The artist first paints solid areas of colour and then dots patterns over the top of these. Next come the dotted lines that **represent the** movement and travel lines across the land. Finally, the lighter colours including white are painted on top of the main shapes to highlight these areas.

Paintings such as this one show stories that are central to Aboriginal community and culture. The symbols are thousands of years old and ensure that these stories are never lost.

inferring

meaning

making meaning or arriving at an answer from, in this case, an image by combining the given information with what is known about the topic

things to know

Different inferences can be made from the same image as the amount of background information is not the same in all viewers.

Point of view and a viewer's background can also influence the inferences made.

Making an inference does not involve 'wild guessing' and must be supported by what the image provides. Avoid straying too far from the image when making inferences.

graphic organiser for inferring

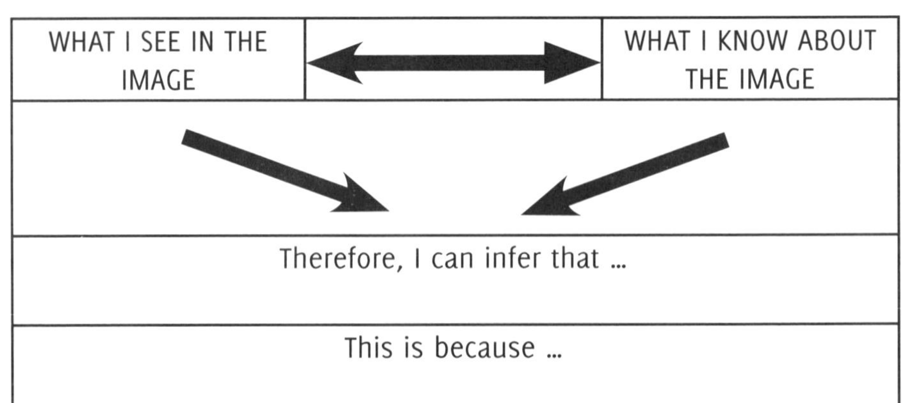

sentence starters

From this data, it can be clearly inferred that ...
The ... (visual image) allows us to infer that ...
The relationship between aspects of ... and ... includes ...
A number of inferences are possible when viewing this ... (visual image).
A viewer can make several inferences from the ... (visual image).
The most likely inference is ...
The ... (visual images/s) provide/s valuable insight into ...
... are commonly understood to mean ...
Therefore, the ... (visual image) means/indicates ...
In addition, ... allows/permits/indicates/supports ...
This ... (visual image) successfully conveys several meanings, each of which ...
It is reasonable to assume ...
My interpretation of ... is supported by ...
The ... (visual image) shows ... and this means ...
... reveals a great deal about the topic, especially ...
Even though it is not directly stated, it is apparent that ...
It could be inferred that the ...
... is especially significant for the insight it provides into ...
For this reason, it could be assumed that ...
... therefore, a plausible inference is ...
Most agree that ...
Inferential methods are used to ...
Given ... it is most likely that ...

example 1

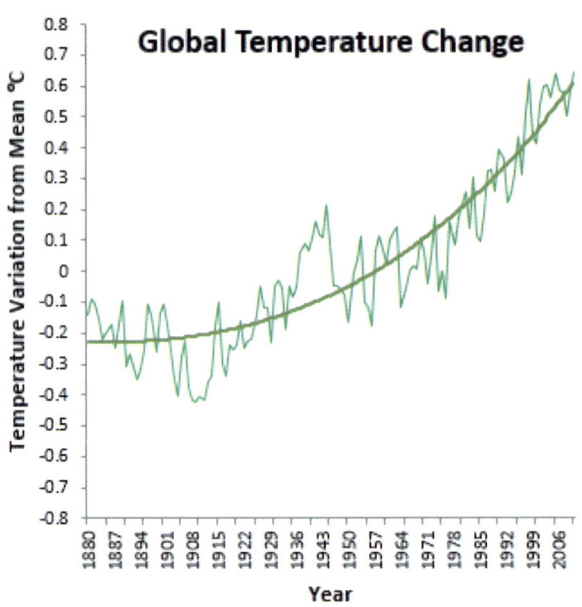

Global temperatures are measured using records since 1880 from a worldwide network of weather stations. That data is compared to the mean global temperatures between 1951 and 1980 to obtain a variation from the mean. The variation is plotted as a green line in the graph above. The graph shows large short-term changes in global temperatures, for example a fall of 0.4°C between 1943 and 1950. However, in the longer term there is a clear pattern of increasing temperatures, indicated by the green trend line.

Global climate change is usually a slow process. Analysis of Antarctic ice cores that go back 440 000 years reveals cycles of ice ages caused by global temperatures that were more than 6°C less than now. These ice ages have occurred on average every 80 000 years. In contrast, an increase of 0.6°C in the trend of global temperatures in the past 40 years, shown in the graph, is a rapid change.

From this data, **it can be clearly inferred that** recent increases in global temperatures are not part of the natural cycles of warming and cooling. What, then, is the cause of the recent rapid increase in temperatures? Laboratory experiments show that increases in atmospheric carbon dioxide levels cause an increase in temperatures (called the greenhouse effect). However, there is a limit to what can be done in the laboratory. **Inferential methods have been used** by scientists to provide an explanation. **Most now agree that** the ever-increasing amount of carbon dioxide emitted by our industrialised world is the likely cause of the recent global warming.

Note: The factual information used in this example is from the California Space Institute (CalSpace) of the University of California (http://earthguide.ucsd.edu/virtualmuseum/climatechange2/01_1.shtml). The inferences are the authors'.

example 2

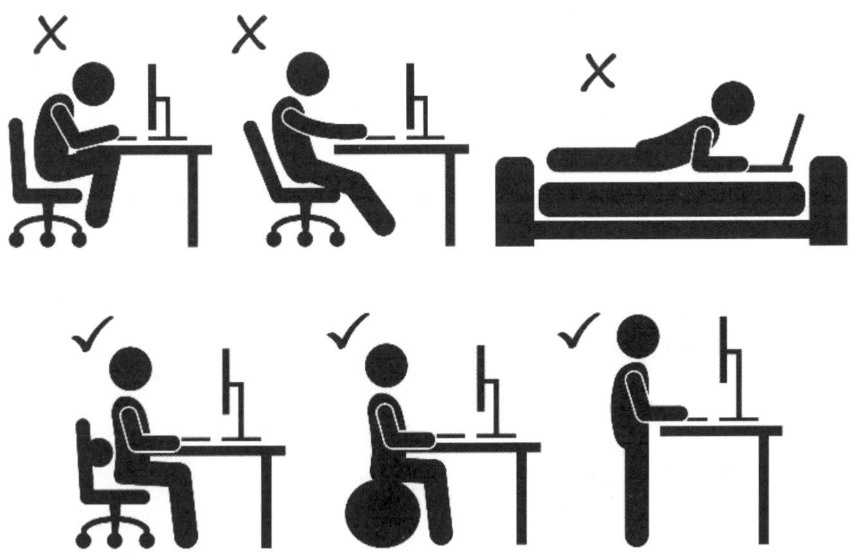

A viewer can make several inferences from this series of diagrams. Even though there are no words to convey information, powerful messages are communicated through the choice of diagrams. **They provide a valuable insight into** correct posture and equipment for the safe use of technology, specifically when working with computers. Ticks **are commonly understood to mean** something is correct, whereas crosses indicate that something is not. **Therefore, the** three **elements** at the top indicate incorrect posture when using a computer. For example, the user will slump in the chair when the computer is too low. Poor back support, either from leaning back in a chair or lying down on a couch, may lead to problems later in life.

Correct posture is demonstrated by the three elements at the bottom of the illustration. Ensure correct posture at a screen by aligning the top of the computer screen with the user's eyes so that there is no slumping. Lower the chair or raise the screen to achieve this. Chairs that provide back support, or equipment that forces the user to maintain a straight back, are much better than those that encourage poor posture. **In addition**, by lowering or raising the height of the desk (many workplaces now have these desks installed), the user can spend time standing up when working at the computer. This can limit the impact on the body of staying sedentary for too long.

example 3

This cartoon **allows us to infer** that the woman who is kneeling and protecting a young child is fearful of a large, dark and ominous-looking figure in the foreground. **The relationship between** the black shape and the other two figures is one of menace and fear.

Colours used in this image, that of warm yellow, orange, dark red, black and white, evoke a hot and fearful emotion. **It could be inferred that the** figure is standing in a doorway with light streaming in and over the woman and child, showing their innocence. **It is reasonable to assume** the woman and child are in trouble.

Overall, this picture reveals it is from the horror genre. The viewer sees the emotion of horror and panic in the woman and child as they are dominated by the antagonist, who is in the form of a dark, monster-like creature. The lighter colours of white and yellow represent good and innocent people, while the evil character is shown using the colour black, **therefore a plausible inference is** that this visual image represents the power of evil over good.

example 4

A number of inferences are possible when viewing this photograph. **Given** the style of clothing, **it is most likely that** the legs hanging over the edge of a tall building in a large city are those of a young man. The camera shot places the viewers in the action, as if they are sitting on the edge. Without seeing the emotion on the person's face, it is difficult to know if the person is frightened or excited.

It could be inferred that the person is adventurous or an 'adrenaline junkie', not suicidal, due to the brightness of the photograph and the colours used in the cityscape. It is certainly not dark and ominous. **For this reason, it could be assumed that** the person is not about to jump off the edge; the photograph does not instil fear in the viewer but rather excitement.

Even though it is not directly stated, there are links between the visual image and the recent phenomenon of Marvel and/or DC movies about superheroes. The figure could be the superhero incognito prior to changing into a crime-fighting character.

This photograph **successfully conveys several meanings, each of which** evokes excitement and adventure due to its brightness and daytime setting.

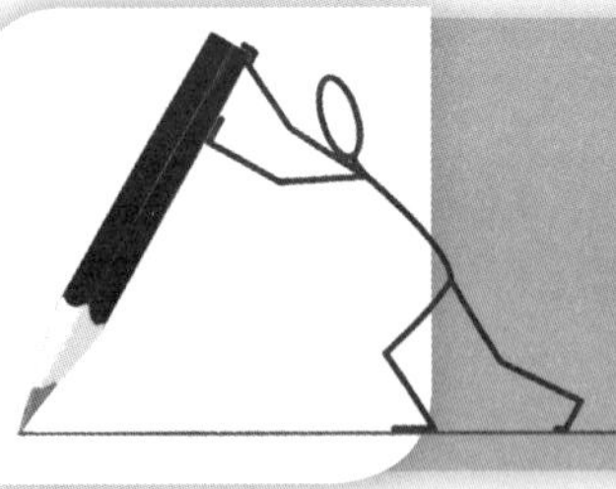

interpreting

meaning

examining a visual image and explaining its meaning or significance, often from a particular point of view

things to know

An interpretation of a visual image often starts with a description of that image and a discussion of its purpose. It then explains the meaning and importance of the different parts of the visual image and how they interact. The conclusion might consider how well the visual image achieves its purpose and/or how the visual image might be used.

graphic organiser for interpreting

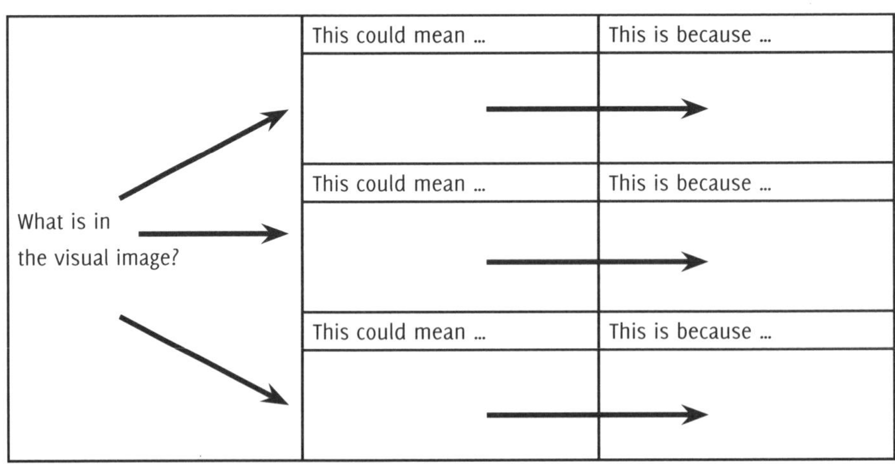

sentence starters

In other words, ...
It follows that ...
There is a clear trend/skew in the data ...
This is unsurprising, given the ...
This confirms the skewed nature of the data ...
This/that makes it difficult to assess ...
This ... (visual image) shows/does not show ...
The purpose of the ... (visual image) is to show the ...
This ... (visual image) can/should not be used to find ...
The ... (visual image) is not a ... because it does not include ...
In this ... (visual image) the artist has contrasted ...
... are synonymous with ...
The ... heightens the viewer's response ...
The artist juxtaposes ... to highlight ...
The juxtaposition of the image within the ... (visual image) could suggest that ...
This provides a valuable insight into/indicates a sense of ...
Because ..., meaning is constructed in this ... (visual image) through the ...
This can be interpreted to mean that ...
... is a significant idea/emotion in the ... (visual image).
While it is clear that this ... (visual image) shows ..., an interpretation is difficult to make because ...
Factors that interfere with an interpretation of this ... (visual image) include ...
There are several interpretations of ...; however, the most common one is ...
A more radical interpretation of ... is ...
A common but incorrect interpretation is ...
It is also unsuitable as ...
... further contributes to ...

example 1

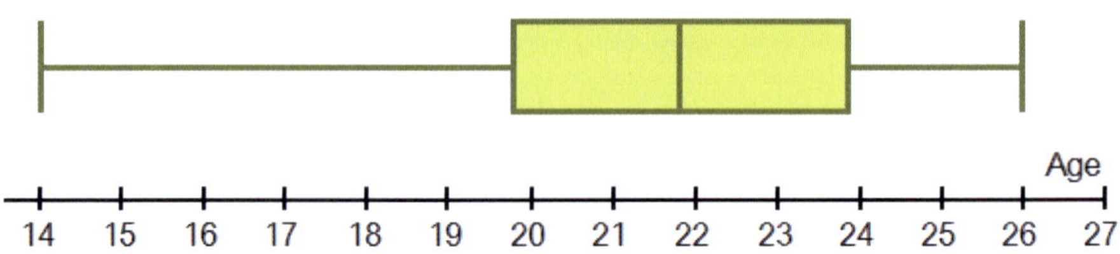

This box-and-whisker plot **shows** the ages of young drink-drivers arrested in Queensland during the years 2010–11. The far left and right sections of the graph (called the *whiskers*) show the ages of the youngest and oldest in the group. The youngest person arrested for drink-driving in that time period was 14 – well below the legal driving age of 17 and the legal drinking age of 18. The oldest in this group appears to be 26, but given the title of the graph, is likely to be 25 – possibly a few days before his or her 26th birthday.

The shaded yellow centre section of the graph (called the *box*) shows the ages of the middle half of the group. **In other words,** half the drink-drivers arrested were aged between almost 20 and nearly 24. **It follows that** the youngest 25% of the group was aged between 14 and 19 and the oldest 25% was 24 years and older. **There is a clear skew in the data** towards the older drivers, with three-quarters of drink-drivers aged 19 years and older. **This is unsurprising, given the** legal minimum driving age of 17 and the legal minimum drinking age of 18.

The median age of young people arrested for drink-driving in Queensland is shown by the line in the middle of the yellow box, that is, nearly 22. The median is more than halfway through the range of 14 to just under 26. **This confirms the skewed nature of the data** mentioned earlier.

While the box-and-whisker plot shows the age distribution of younger drink-drivers, it does not show how many there were. **That makes it difficult to assess the** magnitude of the drink-driving problem. Limiting the graph to those under 26 also restricts the ability to consider the data in the context of the wider population.

example 2

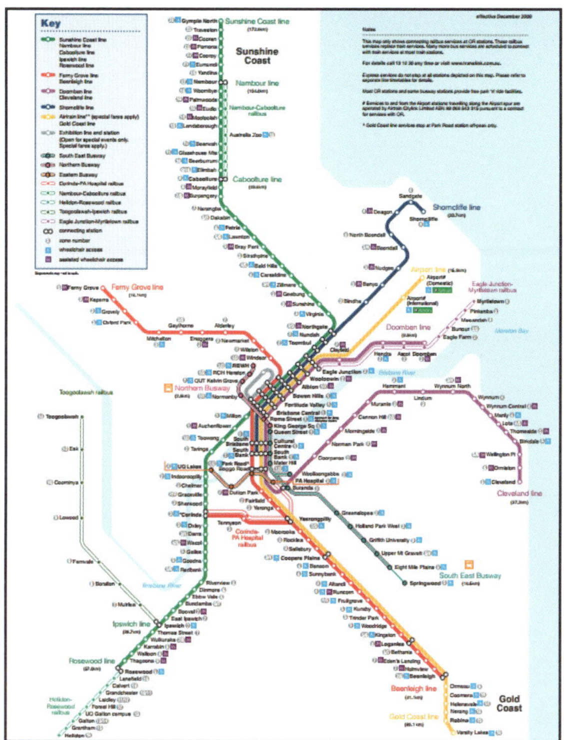

The diagram of the suburban rail network in southeast Queensland shows the arrangement of railway lines and stations, and connections with some bus routes. The six railway lines are shown radiating out from Brisbane Central station, marked with solid colours and labels at the end of each line, and also in the key. Bus routes that connect with the railway lines are shown in the same colour, but do not use solid lines. Train stations and bus stops are marked with white dots.

The purpose of this diagram is to show the connections between the different parts of the railway network and bus routes. For example, to travel between Nudgee and Geebung stations a passenger has to travel on the Shorncliffe line towards Brisbane Central station and then change trains at Northgate station to the Caboolture line travelling away from Brisbane Central station. This line passes through Geebung, where the passenger can disembark.

The diagram is not a map because **it does not include** a scale. Therefore, it does not show the distances between stations or the time taken to travel between stations. Furthermore, there is no compass arrow indicating north. However, the Sunshine Coast line that goes towards the top of the diagram does generally lie to the north of Brisbane Central station and the Gold Coast line heading to the lower right of the diagram does lie to the southeast of Central station.

This diagram **can be used to find** the connections between stations and bus stops, but should not be used to find the distance or direction between different parts of the rail network. **It is also unsuitable as** a guide for travelling around Brisbane on foot or by car.

example 3

In this photograph **the artist has contrasted** the two women sitting on the bench with the information on the store's outside wall. The Adidas logo as well as the active sportspeople **are synonymous with** health and fitness whereas the two women are overweight and, on this occasion, inactive.

The moment could be considered as both a private and a public one because there are just two people, with the camera shot from behind, so we feel a part of the image even though it is taken in a public place.

The body language of the women **heightens the viewer's response** in feeling empathy, as they both have slouched shoulders and are looking at their reflections in the glass wall. **This indicates a sense of** contemplation and sadness.

The artist juxtaposes the healthy and fit images of the sportspeople on the wall with the women who are overweight and obese **to highlight this** contrast. Another feature is that the two figures are sitting on one end of the bench like a set of scales, implying an unbalanced lifestyle.

Because a lack of exercise can lead to poor health and obesity, **meaning is constructed** in this photograph **through the** contrast of healthy and unhealthy lifestyles.

example 4

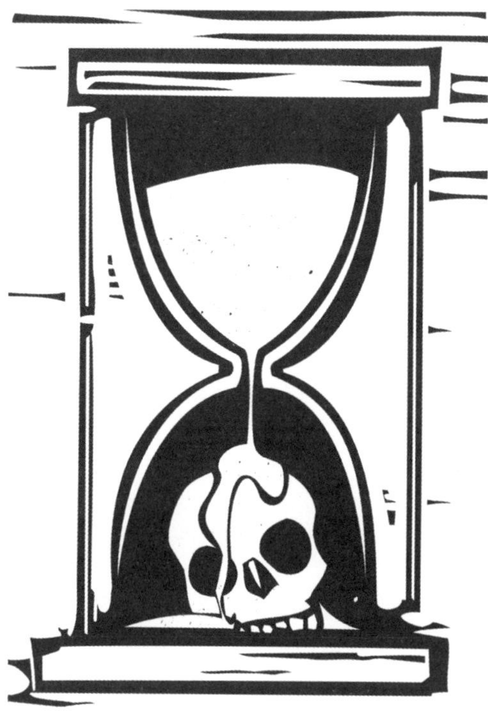

This black and white sketch is based on an hourglass, an old-fashioned device for measuring time. An hourglass comprises two compartments with a small gap between them. It contains sand that slowly runs from the upper to the lower half until it has all flowed through the narrow gap in the middle. Once the bottom half is full, then the hourglass can be turned over to start the next period of time. Before the advent of clocks, these devices were used for measuring different amounts of time by changing the size of the hourglass and the amount of sand.

In this sketch, there is a human skull in the lower part of the hourglass. The skull **is a symbol of** death and the hourglass synonymous with the passage of time. **The juxtaposition of the** skull **within the** hourglass **could suggest that** time is running out for the human race. The expression *the sands of time are running out* **suggests that** there is not much time to do something, so this sketch confirms this sense of doom and gloom. There is global concern that the world's population has outstripped the capacity of planet earth to support it. Resources are diminishing and the planet is getting warmer because of the increased emission of greenhouse gases.

As the sands of time run slowly through the hourglass, the human skull will disappear from view. **This can be interpreted to mean that** if humans continue with the rapid rate of destruction of the planet's resources then all evidence of human existence will be obliterated. The starkness of this black and white visual image **further contributes to** the pessimism that this image conveys.

comparing

meaning

identifying the ways in which two or more representations are similar *and* different

things to know

When comparing visual information, there are several possible approaches: comparing information given in different parts of the same visual image; comparing representations of an idea in a visual image with those in a written text; and comparing two or more visual images. The following pages provide examples of each of these.

A comparison is not a parallel description; that is, avoid writing about one representation and then writing about another. The best way to avoid a parallel description is to structure the text around the attributes/qualities/properties/features of the representations being compared.

When planning a comparison, it can be helpful to sort your ideas using a three-column Venn diagram. For each attribute being compared, three columns are used to list the similarities and differences between the two representations. The overlapping central column is used to show similarities and the differences are shown in the columns that do not overlap (see below the graphic organiser for comparing).

Comparative adjectives are also a feature of comparisons (e.g. slower and slowest; faster and fastest; cleaner and cleanest; quicker and quickest).

graphic organiser for comparing

ATTRIBUTE/FEATURE/ CHARACTERISTIC	IMAGE 1/TEXT 1 DIFFERENCES	SIMILARITIES	IMAGE 2/TEXT 2 DIFFERENCES

sentence starters

Not only ..., but ...

However, ...

Despite the ...

In contrast/a similar way ...

In both cases ...

... (visual images) use similar ...

Obvious differences exist between ... (visual image) and ... (visual image), and these are ...

The main similarity/difference between ... (visual image) and ... (visual image) is ...

There are several ways in which ... (visual image) and ... (visual image) are similar, including ...

A comparison of the elements of ... (visual image) and ... (visual image) shows/reveals ...

Specific differences exist between ... and ...

... and ... are different in a number of respects, especially ...

This significant part of the ... (visual image) highlights the contrast between ... and ...

The similarities between ... (visual image) and ... (visual image) are more significant than their differences.

Several comparisons can be made between ... (visual image) and ... (visual image).

The elements of ... and ... will be compared with ...

This differs from ...

On the other hand, ...

The use of similar ...

... whereas ...

example 1

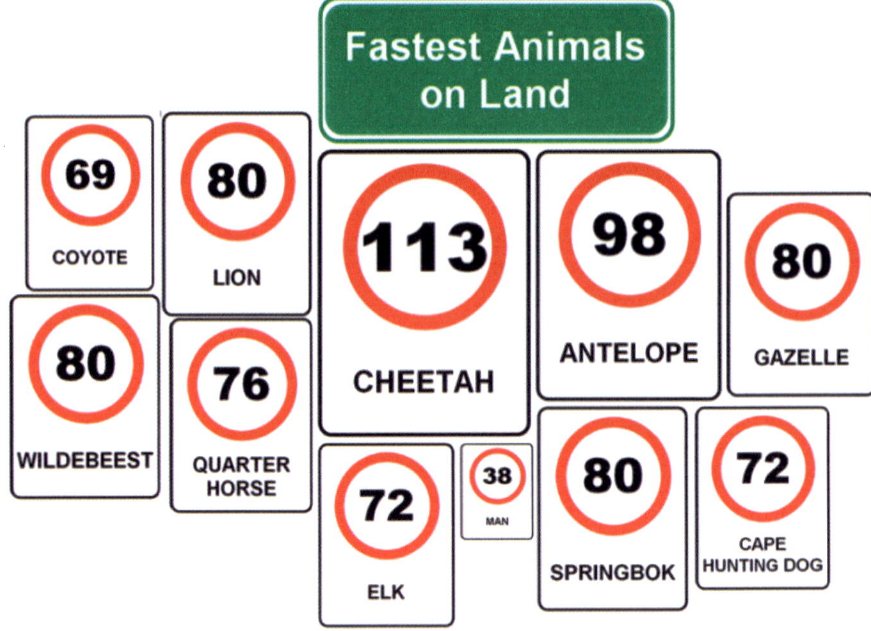

Traffic speed signs have been used creatively in this visual image to contrast the maximum speeds of various animals, including humans (identified on the sign as *man*). **Not only** is the speed shown as a number on the signs, **but** the sizes of the speed signs are proportional to the speeds. The visual image does not show which measurement unit has been used to measure the speeds. **However**, a check of the world record times for sprinting suggests that the speeds in this diagram are measured in kilometres per hour.

A comparison of the elements reveals that the sign representing the cheetah is the largest and contains the highest number, indicating that the cheetah is the fastest land animal on earth. The cheetah can reach speeds up to 113 kilometres per hour. The antelope is the second fastest land animal by a clear margin. However, after these two animals, there is a group of animals that can reach speeds of 70 to 80 kilometres per hour. **In contrast to** these animals, humans are slow, reaching less than half the speed of many of the other animals.

In a race between the animals shown in this diagram, the cheetah would finish first, well ahead of the antelope. There would then be a group of many animals, with a tie between the wildebeest, lion, gazelle and springbok for third place. Humans would finish a long way behind these animals in a poor last place.

example 2

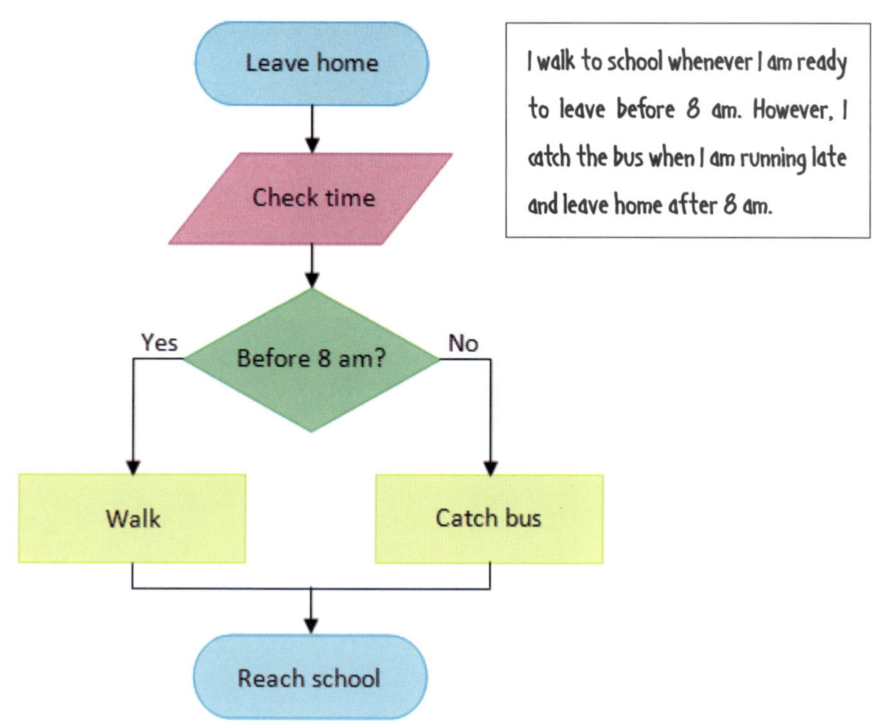

The two sentences in the text box (above right) describe how a student travels to school. The same process is represented visually in the flowchart (above left). **In both cases** the process is codified using the written symbols and vocabulary of the English language. **However**, the flowchart also employs codes in the form of shapes and lines.

The process of travelling to school is described in the written text using 27 words, **whereas** the flowchart uses only 13 words. Despite the additional words, most readers would find the written text easier to interpret than the visual representation in the flowchart. This is because the flowchart requires the reader to understand the meaning of the shapes and the connecting lines. In this example, the flowchart uses ovals to show the start and end of a process, parallelograms to indicate the input or output of information, diamonds to represent a decision and rectangles to denote an action or process. Additionally, the lines incorporate arrowheads to show the order of the various steps.

Flowcharts are used to deconstruct a complex process into individual steps. The identification of the individual steps is the first step in automating a process, for example in a computer program or the electronic instructions that control a bank of lifts. **In contrast,** the steps described in the written text are often combined and reordered, making automation more difficult.

example 3

These two photographs feature houses. Although they have similar subject matter, they evoke different emotions. The first house is shown in a woodland setting while the second is in a rural setting. **Several comparisons can be made** between the two photographs.

Close inspection shows that the house in the first photograph uses limited light and fog to convey a dark and eerie impression. It reminds the viewer of a typical haunted house with the feeling of mystery and perhaps even fear. **In contrast**, the second photograph is taken on a bright, sunny day, bathing the building in light and encouraging the viewer to feel happy and at peace.

Another critical factor that makes these photographs different is the use of colour – with brighter colours used in the second photograph and dark monotones in the first. The use of red paint on the second house creates a warm and welcoming feeling, unlike the first house, which does not seem at all inviting. **Specific differences also exist between** the photos with respect to the inclusion of everyday objects. The cow, the windmill and the fence in the colourful image all contribute to the welcoming impression, **whereas** the first photograph has no similar features.

The use of similar subject matter – houses in country settings – serves to heighten the contrast in emotion. The **obvious differences that exist between** the two images, such as the use of colour, light and shade, have a significant impact on the intended meanings.

example 4

This picture draws attention to the typical representation of home or domestic life in the late 1950s – probably in America. At that time, the roles of men and women were clearly defined. The wife and mother stayed at home and was a full-time homemaker. She cooked and cleaned, took care of the children, and ensured that all her husband's needs were met. **On the other hand**, the husband worked outside the home and was the 'breadwinner', that is, he was the sole income earner.

A comparison of the elements of this picture reveals much about the time. The man and the little girl are doing, presumably, what they want to be doing. He is relaxing on the couch, reading a book and smoking his pipe. The television was a recent addition to many homes at that time and the little girl watches it intently. She **is also** relaxing. The woman, **on the other hand**, is working hard. She is vacuuming the carpet and holding up the couch with a single hand. This represents the extraordinary effort needed to be a perfect homemaker. It also suggests that the woman is supporting her husband by doing all the household duties for him. **In a similar way**, he supports her financially. Unlike men, many women did not have financial independence at that time.

All members of the family are smartly dressed. Advice to women at the time was to smarten themselves up so that they looked attractive when they welcomed their husbands home from work. The woman in the picture has clearly done this; she has combed her hair, changed her clothes and applied fresh make-up. The high heels give a hint of glamour **in contrast to** her mundane existence. The child and the mother are dressed in pink – a feminine colour. The child is in a pretty dress with a matching ribbon in her hair, indicating that she is in training for the role her mother plays. The man is also smartly dressed, probably in his business or office clothes although he appears to be wearing slippers.

The pink colour is repeated in the walls, suggesting that the décor has been chosen by the wife. However, the viewer's eyes are drawn to the most unusual part of the picture, that is, where the woman's hand is holding up the couch. **This significant part of the picture highlights the contrast between** the roles of men and women at the time.

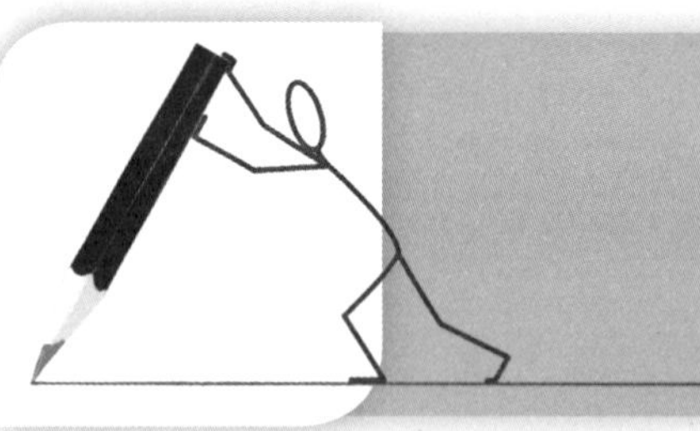

analysing

meaning

examining the parts of something in detail and discussing or interpreting the relationship of the parts to each other and to the whole

things to know

As analysing may involve describing, comparing, explaining, interpreting and critiquing, the information on those pages may also be useful.

graphic organiser for analysing

- describe the part
- discuss its relationship to other parts and the whole image

- describe the part
- discuss its relationship to other parts and the whole image

PART OF THE IMAGE

PART OF THE IMAGE

PART OF THE IMAGE

PART OF THE IMAGE

- describe the part
- discuss its relationship to other parts and the whole image

- describe the part
- discuss its relationship to other parts and the whole image

sentence starters

The ... (visual image) shows the/that ...
For simplicity, it illustrates ...
The elements of the ... (visual image) show that ...
This ... (visual image) represents/suggests that ...
... is/are represented by the connections between ...
... indicate/indicates/demonstrate/demonstrates ...
It also reflects ...
In this example/For example, ...
It is useful to appreciate ... as this can ...
The/This ... (visual image) can be used to ...
The artist has used a range of textures to create ...
Together the/these ... suggest a ...
In analysing this ... (visual image), a message that can be inferred is ...
... also contributes to ...
... could indicate a ...
This is suggested/emphasised by ...
The ... (visual image) gives useful information to/about/for ...
The artist/creator of the ... (visual image) shows ...
... and this interpretation has been achieved by ...
The artist has positioned ...
All the elements combine to illustrate/create a powerful message, which is ...
The artist is giving the viewer an insight into/trying to tell us ...
... could be broken down in the following way/s:
... effectively combines ... and ...
There is very little relationship between ... and ...
The main contribution that ... makes to the meaning is ...
The ... demonstrates ...

example 1

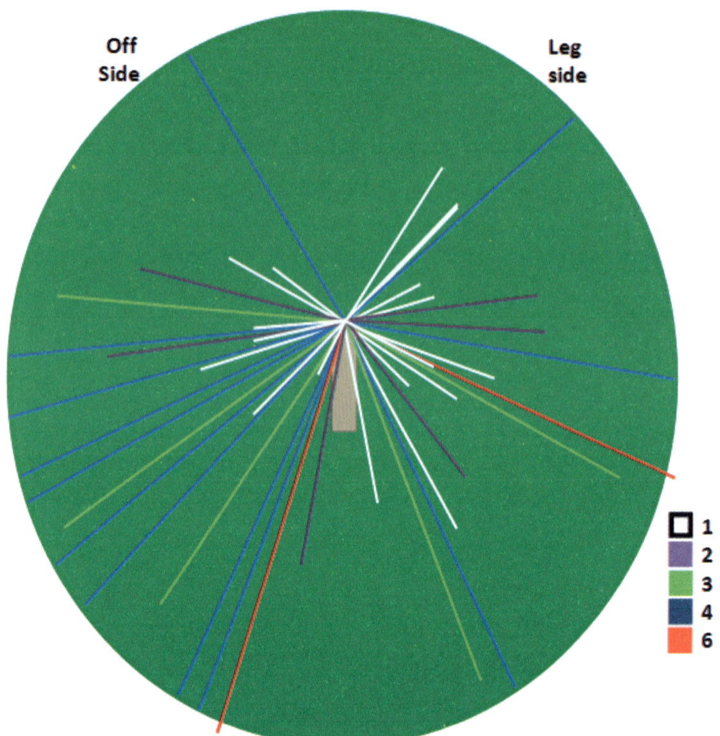

The cricket wagon wheel diagram **shows the** scoring strokes played in an innings by a batter. **For simplicity, it illustrates** the strokes relative to the place where the batter stands. Although players bat from both ends of the wicket, **in this diagram** the position of the batter **is always shown** at the upper end of the wicket. Each line **represents** those strokes where the batter scored runs, with colour used to show the number of runs scored. The angle and length of each line show the direction that the ball was hit and the distance travelled by the ball before it was fielded.

The elements of the diagram show that there is a good spread of boundaries and lower scoring shots. This batter scored 14 boundaries (two of them were sixes), five strokes that resulted in three runs, two runs on six occasions and 18 singles, for a total of 105 runs. Of the scoring shots, 72% were in front of the wicket and only 28% behind the wicket. More runs (54%) were scored on the off side. **This suggests that** the batter's strength is driving the ball.

The wagon wheel diagram **gives** an opposition captain **useful information for** deciding where to place the fielders. A strong off side field **is indicated** for this batter. A batting coach can also use the diagram to determine which shots the batter needs to work on. The diagram **suggests that** this batter could practise more leg side scoring shots.

Together, the number and distribution of the scoring strokes **suggest a** very accomplished batter.

example 2

This model **represents** a water molecule. It shows the three-dimensional arrangement of the two atoms of hydrogen (white balls) and one atom of oxygen (red ball) that together form the molecule. Strong electrical forces hold the atoms together, **represented by the connections between** the balls. The model clearly shows why the molecular formula of water is H_2O.

Although not constructed to scale, the size of the balls **indicates** that oxygen is a larger atom than hydrogen. **The** model **demonstrates** that the molecule has some internal space and shows the approximate distance between the atoms. **It also reflects the** valency rules that are used in science. **In this example** oxygen has a valency of two (demonstrated by the two connections) and hydrogen of one (shown by the single connection).

Like many models used to simplify complex ideas, this model is not entirely accurate. Atoms are not spherical, solid objects and they are not held together by physical connections.

It is useful to appreciate the shapes of molecules **as this can** help us to understand their physical properties. **This** model **can be used to** show how water molecules can be stacked in different ways **and helps explain why** water expands as it freezes.

Molecular models such as this are often used to show the arrangements of the atoms in molecules. It is common for hydrogen to be represented as a white ball and oxygen in red. Other colours are used for other types of atoms. Some models can be very complex: a model of DNA contains thousands of atoms.

example 3

This digital artwork displays a futuristic scene with a dark and dreary world in the background and a robot form in the right foreground of the image. It appears that the picture was created using computer technology.

The artist has used a range of textures to create an unsettled feeling in the work. **For example**, the bottom third of the image depicts a rough, scratchy and dark grey surface. Next are some shapes that show different-levelled buildings in a lighter grey but with the same rough technique as used in the lower part of the image. The sky is pale, moving towards a textured pale blue framing the top part of the image. **Together these** features **suggest a** post-apocalyptic world.

In the foreground, the artist has featured a personified robot form. The robot is created from everyday objects such as an old-style television and an old toaster. On top of the head is a single antenna and two circular disks placed on the front representing the robot's eyes. The viewer's eyes are drawn to the head and eyes of the robot and this evokes strong emotion.

In analysing this picture, a message that can be inferred is that the robot is sad and depressed, indicated by the top part of the body being slightly tilted down. The eye on the right also has a lid that is half closed. The misery of the robot is obvious to the viewer from its body language.

The background of the artwork **also contributes to** the feeling of wretchedness as there is an absence of colour, showing an unhealthy environment. The tinge of blue in the sky, however, **could indicate a** sense of hope for the world.

example 4

This illustration shows three girls of school age. The two in the background are talking to each other in conspiratorial tones **and this is suggested by** their postures. Their hands are covering their mouths and the other girl's back is turned. This is a common way to represent people whispering to each other hurtful and harmful remarks about someone else. Their smiles are those of malice towards the girl in the foreground, who is clearly unhappy and gains no pleasure from being near the other girls.

The artist shows the isolation of the girl cast in the role of the victim and this is emphasised by the difference in her appearance. She has a downturned mouth, and her eyes are positioned to one side as she gazes nervously around her, perhaps mindful that the gossiping might turn to something more serious. Only the victim is in a strong colour, whereas the other girls are in greenish/grey tones, and this highlights her exclusion. The choice of a sombre colour palette emphasises her despondency.

The bullies are intimidating **and this interpretation has been achieved by** the long menacing shadows that are much larger than the shadow cast by the girl in the foreground. **The artist has positioned** the large shadows in such a way that they appear to close in around the outcast. This suggests she is trapped in the lonely world of the victim. Her shadow is also narrower, so in terms of the power relationship, she is much weaker.

All the elements combine to create a powerful message, which is that bullying has destructive power. The outcast's world is a miserable one that chips away at her self-confidence. It is painful for her to go to school. She stands for all the children who are bullied, especially in school. **The artist is giving the viewer an insight into** bullying; it excludes the victim from the group at a time of life when belonging really matters.

critiquing

meaning

analysing something in detail, often assessing or evaluating what is presented

things to know

When planning a critique, the parts of the image should be examined and the way these parts interact is also important. Focusing on the strengths and weaknesses of what is presented also forms part of a critique. Significant background knowledge is required, especially where conflicting points of view are evident.

A critique (noun) is a detailed and analytical evaluation of something.

graphic organiser for critiquing

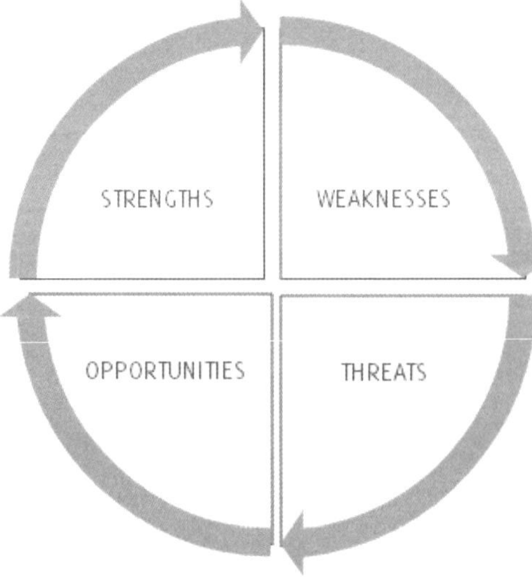

sentence starters

However, ... has/have been allowed to distort ...

... prompts the viewer to/suggests ...

This approach suggests that ...

The (features) tell a different story.

There is a clear incompatibility between ...

A further problem in understanding this (visual image) is the ...

It is not clear what is ...

A different layout, such as ... would rectify this misinterpretation.

The conflict/debate between the ... and the ... makes it unsuitable for ...

The ... (visual image) implies that ...

However, the ... (visual image) does not distinguish between ... and ...

There are significant benefits/advantages from ...

Some experts question the emphasis on ...

Absent from the image is any indication that ...

The ... (visual image) depicts the relationship between ... and ...

The artist has highlighted the ...

The issue of ... can be viewed from several different perspectives.

The ... (visual image) presents only part of the issue/debate; missing from the ... (visual image) is the ... (view/perspective/opinion)

The image gives more weight to ... than ...

Creators of the ... (visual image) want the reader to view it in a particular way, namely ...

There has been much/little criticism of ...

Using the ... (visual image) to inform decisions is fraught with problems/worth doing because ...

The perspective of ... has been overlooked.

Therefore, it could be argued that ...

example 1

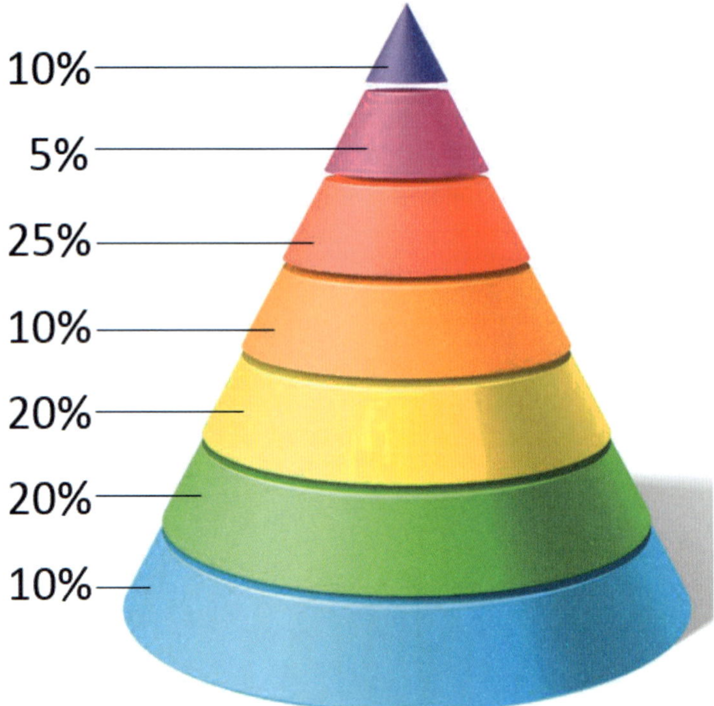

Information is presented in this conical graph in two ways. First, the cone is divided into seven horizontal slices. Second, there are annotations that use percentages to show the amount in each category. The graph is simple and visually appealing. **However**, these artistic considerations **have been allowed to distort** the presentation of the data. This is illustrated by separately considering the two methods of presenting the data.

The division of the cone into coloured slices **prompts the viewer to** interpret the graph based on the size of each slice. **This approach suggests that** the categories are arranged in descending order of size, moving from bottom to top. Furthermore, the change in the size of each slice implies that the categories decrease in an even, proportional way.

The annotations **tell a different story.** They show that the largest category is the red slice, representing one quarter of the whole. The categories are not arranged in order of size, nor does there appear to be a consistent relationship between them. **There is a clear incompatibility between** the size of each slice and the corresponding percentage.

A further problem in understanding this graph **is the** absence of any information that explains its purpose. **It is not clear what is** being measured and what each slice represents. **An** informative title and a key for the colour coding **could rectify this problem.**

The conflict between the visual representation **and the** annotations and the lack of information about the purpose of the graph **make it an unsuitable** method of presenting data.

example 2

A food pyramid is a triangular – or pyramid-shaped – diagram used universally to inform healthy eating and spread nutritional advice. The triangular shape and the arrangement of the food **suggest** some foods are 'good' and some 'bad'. At the bottom of the pyramid is the bread, grains, pasta and rice group (carbohydrates). **The** diagram **implies that** foods from this group should be the bulk of what we eat. **However, the diagram does not distinguish between** *whole grains,* which are very good for us, and *refined grains,* which are not. The diagram also implies that foods at the top of the image from the fats, oils and sweets group should be consumed sparingly.

Following the advice that this pyramid conveys can lead to health problems. Dietary fat from healthy sources has been shown to have a number of beneficial effects. It can increase weight loss, reduce the risk of heart disease, lower blood sugars and cholesterol and maintain brain function, especially in children. **There are significant** health **benefits from** consuming oils from plants. Consumption of large amounts of carbohydrates can contribute to weight gain, increase the risk of heart disease and interfere with concentration.

Some health **experts question the emphasis** on dairy consumption, especially whole milk. However, dairy products are near the top of the diagram, giving the impression that their consumption should be low. While dairy products are one of the main sources of calcium – an important mineral for healthy lives – many vegetables and meat sources contain plenty of calcium with fewer kilojoules.

The recommended daily allowance of fruits is two to four servings per day. The position of fruit on the diagram suggests that the amount consumed should be similar to the amount of vegetables eaten. Even though fruit is a natural source of sugar, too much sugar can cause blood sugar levels to peak and fall, creating a roller-coaster ride all day long.

Absent from the image is any indication that physical activity is the other essential ingredient of a healthy lifestyle.

N.B. There are many forms of the food pyramid and it changes as health experts review what is the best combination of foods from the food groups to keep people healthy. This is an older version of the food pyramid. Recent versions present the food groups on a plate.

example 3

This sketch implies a particular relationship between people when colonisation occurs. **The issue of** invasion or settlement **can be viewed from different perspectives. The artist has effectively highlighted** the suppression of the first inhabitants of the land through the use of body language.

There is clear incompatibility between the figures standing and those at a lower level. The white explorers are represented as superior to the Indigenous people, whose actions indicate fear and caution as evidenced by the positioning of their bodies and the use of their arms to shield themselves. The standing figure shows confidence, with one hand in his pocket balanced with the other hand on his sabre.

The placement of the figures represents a difference in power between the coloniser and the colonised, the civilised and the uncivilised. **A different layout, such as** putting the figures on an equal level, **would rectify this misrepresentation**.

This approach suggests that the image's creator was attempting to capture a historic moment in time when the explorers first 'discovered' the new land. **However, it does not take into account** that the land was already inhabited and therefore previously discovered.

example 4

The issue of whether graffiti is art or vandalism **can be viewed from different perspectives.** The designer of this photo has shown the perpetrator of graffiti incognito. This approach suggests that the painter is trying to hide his or her identity and therefore suggests that there is something shameful about graffiti.

This image presents only part of the debate about graffiti. **There has been much criticism of** graffiti, with many people believing that it is vandalism predominantly carried out on private property without permission. Many property owners object to graffiti, especially when the work has little artistic merit. In fact, several graffiti artists/vandals have had to go to court, an example being the Brisbane artist Anthony Lister in 2016.

However, **the perspectives of** the artist and those who appreciate the skill and ability of talented graffiti artists **have been overlooked** in this photograph. There are many examples of graffiti that have artistic merit. In many cases the graffiti artist has considerable talent and some property owners invite them to decorate their walls. Most graffiti is done on rundown buildings and ugly walls, such as the one shown in the photograph, or in disadvantaged areas. Therefore, **it could be argued** that good graffiti improves and beautifies the environment.

The debate between the supporters and critics of graffiti is polarised and **makes** a single photograph **an unsuitable** method of presenting both sides of the argument.

reflecting

meaning

responding in a personal way to a visual image by making personal connections with the information or ideas in that visual image

things to know

Reflective writing about a visual image usually involves a brief description of the image (see pages 6 to 11), an interpretation of the information or ideas presented in the image (see pages 24 to 29), and an explanation of what the information or ideas mean for you (see pages 12 to 17).

Use of the personal pronouns 'I', 'me' and 'my' is acceptable in reflective writing because personal responses are encouraged and respected.

Language choices may be more informal than with other forms of writing.

graphic organiser for reflecting

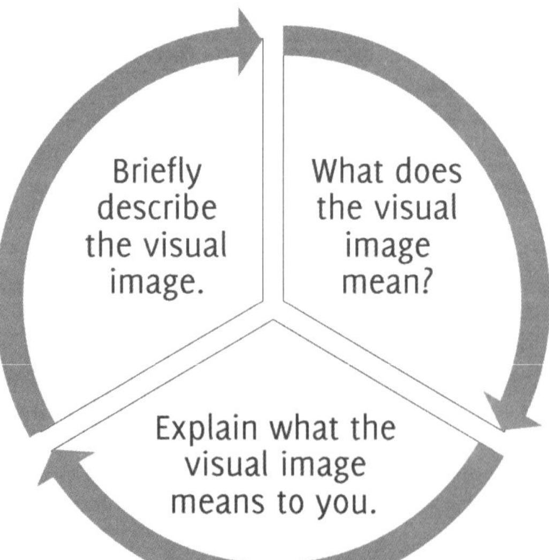

sentence starters

I find that the (visual image) is most easily interpreted if I think of it as ...

I can/cannot see a clear trend in the ...

It seems that there are reasons/factors/circumstances that help to explain ...

I need more information to understand/enable me to ...

I have been provided with sufficient information to enable to me to ...

To make sense of ..., I would need to research ...

When interpreting this (visual image), it is also important to know ...

I was surprised to see that ... because I did not realise that ...

I now understand why ...

It concerns me that/concerned me that ...

I already knew that ...

The ... (visual image) makes me feel ... (insert emotion), as it could be interpreted that ...

I can relate to this ... (visual image) because ...

Now I realise ...

My main response to this ... (visual image) is ...

The ... (visual image) reminds me of the times I ...

The ... (visual image) conjures up several sensations/emotions for me.

I remember the feeling of ...

The ... (visual image) also makes me think of ...

I also/can also remember/recall ...

I loved the .../hated the ...

Using the ... (visual image) to inform decisions is fraught with problems/worth doing because ...

The perspective of ... has been overlooked.

Perhaps it would allow me to see ...

The ... (visual image) immediately suggests to me that ...

My impression is confirmed by ...

example 1

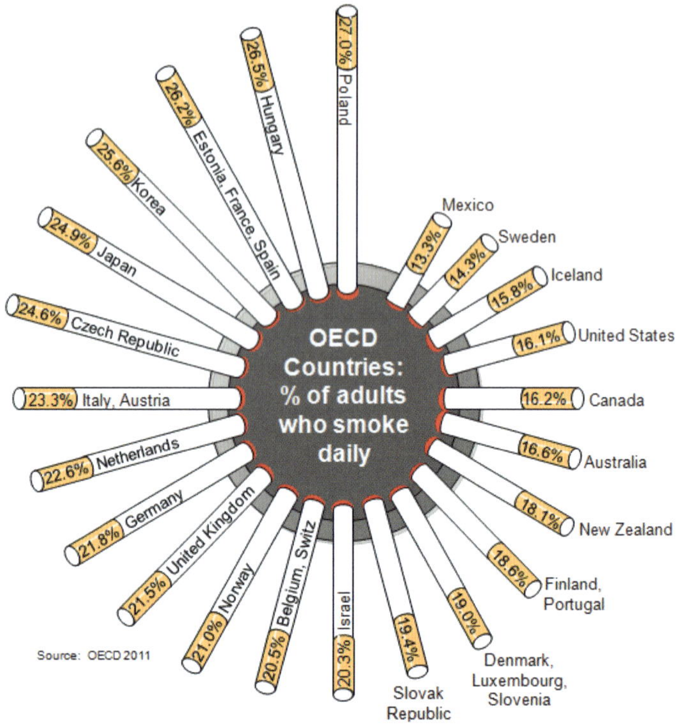

The diagram illustrates the smoking rates of selected countries, showing the percentage of the total adult population who smoke daily. The selected nations are the members of the Organisation for Economic Co-operation and Development (OECD), a group of more highly developed nations. **I find that the** graph **is most easily interpreted if I think of it as** a column graph, although it has a curved axis, rather than the horizontal axis that is more common.

Smoking rates in the selected countries range from 13.3%, in the case of Mexico, to 27.0% in Poland. However, **I cannot see a clear trend in the** information presented in the graph. For example, smoking rates in Sweden and Iceland are below 16%, while those of nearby Scandinavian countries are higher: Finland 18.6%, Denmark 19.0%, and Norway 21.0%. Similarly, smoking rates in Canada, Australia, and New Zealand, ranging from 16.2% to 18.1%, are lower than the rate in the United Kingdom at 21.5% – a nation with many cultural similarities. **It seems that there are factors** affecting smoking rates other than cultural issues or geographic proximity.

I need more information to understand this data. Laws about tobacco advertising and the amount of government taxes on tobacco products would affect the number of people who smoke. Other relevant information would be about government information programs concerning the dangers of smoking and how to quit. **To make sense of the graph I need to research** this information about each country. **Perhaps it would allow me to see** a clearer trend in national smoking patterns.

example 2

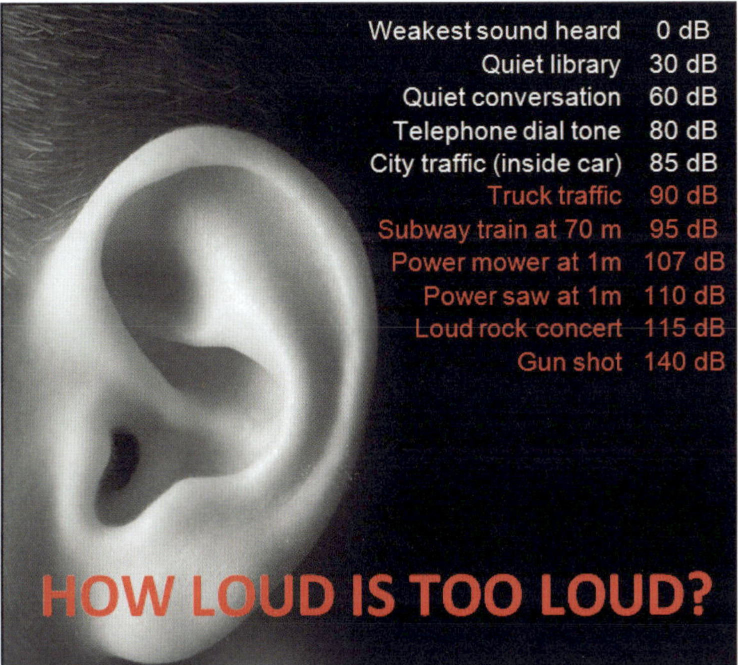

The photograph of a human ear on this chart **immediately suggests to me that** it is about hearing. **My impression is confirmed by** the title at the bottom of the chart. Looking more closely, the written text in the smaller font shows the typical intensity of eleven sounds, measured in decibels (shown in the chart as dB). The sounds that are not harmful to human hearing are shown in white and those where prolonged exposure may damage our hearing are in red. The use of red when everything else is in black and white makes me focus immediately on the harmful sounds.

I know that the information in the chart is based on the generally accepted advice that prolonged exposure to sounds above 85 decibels can be harmful to human hearing. **When interpreting the chart, it is also important to know** that every increase of three decibels in the noise level represents a doubling of the sound intensity.

I was surprised to see that the noise of city traffic heard inside a car is close to the level that can damage our hearing. If that traffic includes frequent trucks, the noise level becomes harmful. The sounds of traffic are a common experience for those living in cities, but **I did not realise that** it could be damaging. **I now understand why** there are high walls separating busy freeways from nearby homes.

It concerns me that prolonged exposure to other common sounds such as power mowers and power saws can also be harmful. My father is often exposed to these sounds. However, the most alarming information is the level of rock concert noise. **I already knew that** the sound levels in a rock concert can be harmful. **Now I realise** that at 115 decibels, rock concert noise is 30 decibels, or ten times, more than the safe noise level.

example 3

This image includes two photos, one of a man and one of a boy, most likely taken some time ago as they are both wearing older style uniforms and the photos are in black and white. They are being held in the hands of an older woman.

To make sense of the photo, **I would need to research** the history of war and in particular soldiers' uniforms. I can see that these two images could be the same person as the uniforms look like they are from different time periods.

The visual image makes me feel sad **as it could be interpreted that** the images are of the woman's husband as a soldier and as a boy in the cadets, possibly now killed in a war. Judging by her hands, the woman is considerably older than the two figures, so she could be reminiscing about the time when he was alive and with her.

I can relate to this image because my grandfather was a Lieutenant Colonel in World War II. Even though he returned home after the war, I know that his involvement had a great impact on his life. He had been a prisoner of war and was missing in action when my mother was born. **My main response to this image** is to reflect that war can affect people's lives, often in an adverse way and many years later, especially when lives are lost.

example 4

This illustration depicts many people, including families, having fun at the beach. It is a sunny day with a few clouds in the sky. The sand is bright yellow. There is a group of beach houses and restaurants to the right of the sand and sea and a lighthouse in the distance.

The people are involved in activities such as swimming, sailing, beach sports, sunbaking, eating and walking. It feels relaxing. **The picture reminds me of the times** I used to go to the beach with my family, usually during the holidays. **The picture conjures up several sensations for me.** We used to run across the sand in those days. **I remember the feeling of** sand between my toes. On particularly windy days, **I recall** the sand blowing against my legs and stinging my skin.

The picture also makes me think of the sounds of the surf and people having fun and being happy. **I can almost smell** the sand, sea and of course fish and chips. **I also remember** sometimes being sunburnt – something I try to avoid now.

I loved the times we spent at the beach. Looking at pictures like this one makes me nostalgic for the happy times I spent with my family on holiday near the ocean. They were wonderful holidays and I shall never forget them.

useful language when writing about visual images

describing ideas

action: activity behaviour gesture heading to motion movement reaction response slow-motion speed time lapse travel

angle: above aligned anticlockwise below bird's-eye view clockwise counter-clockwise degrees diagonal direction east eye level flat gradient high level low north parallel perpendicular radiate slope south steep tilt west

appearance: air aspect different form identical look manifestation represent stand for style

brightness: bright contrast dark dazzle faint grey light medium mid misty pale shades washed-out

camera shot: above behind bird's-eye view close-up command/ commanding dominate eye level focalisation highlight in front of long shot low mid-shot offer perspective placement viewer

colour: black and white blend bright chromatic clash colourful colourless contrast cool dark depth discolour dominant greyscale harmonise hue light monotone opaque palette pastel predominantly primary range saturation scheme secondary shade shading spectrum technicolour tinge tone translucent transparent warm

composition: arrangement artwork compilation comprise connect contraction creation cross design distribution (of) form format formulation imagery intersect juxtapose layout make-up meaning message miserable object off-centre order overlap painful part position production section setting stand out structure subject technique title work work of art

context: background blurred climate condition detail environment setting sharp silhouette situation

depth: absence deep high level low mid-depth perspective range shallow

emotion: afraid angry annoyed anxious body language cheerful cold comical confident contented creepy dark depressed dreary doom empathy excited evoke fearful feeling frightened fulfilled funny gloomy happy hopeful horror humorous interested intimidated inviting jubilant malicious melancholy mood morbid nostalgia ominous optimistic outcast peaceful pessimistic powerful relaxed sad safe satirical satisfied scary secure shame sombre strong terror uncertain unhappy unsettled warm

feature: annotation aspect attribute characteristic component element facet factor icon/iconic label mark nature object part peculiarity property quality symbol/symbolic subject of trait

framing: arrangement border contain edge/edging encircle enclose engulf include loose masked mount outline salience setting surround/surroundings tight (see also *shape*)

layout and position: above accent accompany advertise along arranged asymmetrical attached background backward base behind bottom central close column complement conceal diametrically disguise dispersed distributed/distribution divided dominant/dominate down end of enhance enrich facing far followed by foreground forward go together halfway hanging harmonise horizontal impact in front of in the distance include influence inner/innermost inside irregular left lies location lower middle near obverse opposite/opposed organised outer/outermost outside part passes through place/placement power/powerful present promote proximity relative reveal reverse right role row running from ... to ... side side-by-side show strong superimposed supplement suspended symmetrical top towards up upper vertical weak

light: absence accent beam dark daytime faint full glow highlight illumination levels low light mid-light night-time ray reveal shadow/shade spotlight sunlight

medium: acrylic board canvas charcoal collage crayon digital etch fabric ink marble metal oil paint paper pastels pen pencil photograph plaster plastic print sculpture silk-screen stone watercolour wax wood

number: absence amount common decimal fewer/fewest fraction groups of lack large less/least limited many more/most multiple nil per cent percentage rare scant scarce small some sum total value whole

pattern: asymmetric axis balanced centre connected even geometric grid middle radiating repeating spiral swirling symmetric tessellation unbalanced uneven

purpose: aim comment on display draw attention to function idea illustrate intention objective point principle rationale reason represent role use

useful language when writing about visual images

representation of subject matter: accurate almost approximately authentic characterise/characteristic code/codify connect denote detailed embody epitomise example/exemplify exploded view generally generic interpretation literal nearly particular portray/portrayal precise realistic show size specific stand (for) stylised symbolic/symbolise synonymous typical

scale: actual enlarged equal equally spaced extent goes from ... to graph key large-scale map mark measured model not to scale proportional ratio reduced represent ruler size small-scale starts with to scale units unscaled

shape and line: asymmetric ball base boundary broken circular circumference concentric congruent conical cross cubic curved cylindrical dashed diamond distort dot/dotted edge elliptical elongate face flat hemispherical hollow intersect irregular line oval parallelogram perimeter point prism pyramid rectangular regular round semi-circular skewed solid spherical square straight symmetric/symmetry three-dimensional triangular truncate two-dimensional

significance: consequence critical essence/essential impact importance/important key magnitude noteworthiness relevance weight/weighting

similarity: alike common compare congruent dissimilar group like shape similar size unlike

size: big declining depth dimension diminishing distance extent growing height high increasing large length little low magnitude maximum minimum proportions quantity reducing short small tall value width

space: area evenly spaced irregular large limited regular small unlimited volume

texture: coarse fine finish jagged matt rough scratchy shiny smooth touch

trend: accompany arrow change changeable clear consistent decline decrease emerge extend fall fast impact increase inverse order rapid rate rise slow steady variable

vector: demands/grabs attention flow guide lead line of sight movement path pattern sequence

visual image: advertisement blueprint box-and-whisker plot caricature cartoon chart demonstration depiction diagram display drawing figure flowchart graph icon illustration image infographic interpretation map musical score network painting pattern photograph picture plan plot portrayal print representation scale drawing sketch symbol tessellation visual aid

connecting ideas

describing: absolutely additionally alike/like/just like along with also although and apart from are as as shown in/by as well as commonly concurrent/concurrently except/exception finally for example for the most part furthermore generally/in general however is composed of is made up of lastly mainly many moreover normally shows some specifically such as too typically ultimately unlike usually

explaining: also and and this leads to because by consequently due to except/exception for for example/instance for this reason generally hence in addition it follows that provided that since so such as then therefore thus when while why

inferring: although apparently as a result of associated with because consequently despite due to even though evidently for example hence however if ... then in addition in other words it appears it is clear might mean provide since specifically therefore this can unless whereas

interpreting: after alternative/alternatively although as then at the same time because consequently despite even though for example/instance furthermore however in addition in particular in that respect instead of nevertheless overall shows since such that is therefore whereas while

comparing: additionally alike/like/just like also alternative/alternatively although and as well as both but differs from except however in all cases/instances in common in contrast to in many cases in most cases in other respects in spite of in the same way not only ... but also on the one hand on the other hand similarly whereas yet

analysing: also although and as well as because combine for example/instance furthermore hence however if ... then in addition in other respects in the same way is made up of not only ... but also on the other hand shows the/that so specifically than the reason for therefore thus unless when yet

critiquing: also another as well at one level because consequently especially even if even though for example/instance hence however implies moreover nevertheless on the contrary on the one hand on the other hand suggests unless

reflecting: additionally alternatively at first at the same time because of furthermore initially means that might be of course perhaps previously subsequently

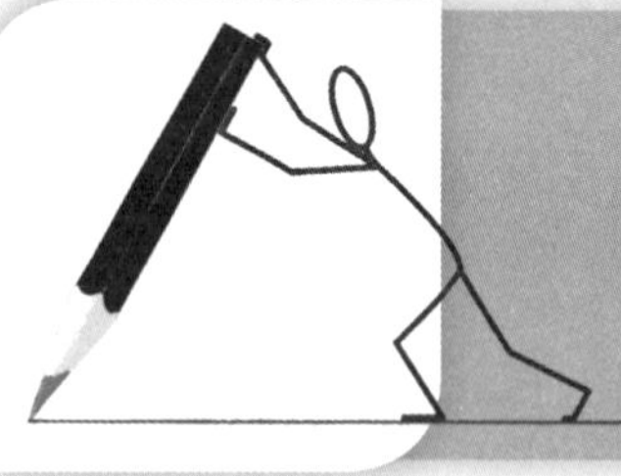

substitutes for 'shows that'

explanation

When writing about visual images, it is necessary to refer to information provided in that image. Relying on phrases such as, 'the graph shows that ...', 'the diagram shows that ...', 'the photograph shows that ...', can be tedious and unsophisticated. The list below provides some alternatives.

ways of saying

according to
affirms that
as can be seen in ...,
confirms that
conveys
demonstrates that
depicts the
displays the
establishes that
exemplifies the
exhibits the
explains that
exposes the
gives the result that
illustrates the idea that
implies that
indicates that
is an example of
is consistent with
it can be seen in ... that
leads to the conclusion that
manifests the
presents the
proves that
provides evidence of
records the
reflects the
represents the
results in
reveals that
suggests that
symbolises
validates the result that

avoiding the use of 'I', 'me' and 'my'

explanation

The use of the first person 'I', 'me' and 'my' is acceptable, in fact desirable when responding to a narrative image, particularly where a personal response is sought. However, when responding to informative texts the use of first person is generally discouraged. Writing in third person gives more authority to the work. In addition, the use of the passive voice (i.e., the 'doer' is removed) is also a prominent feature of more technical texts. The phrases below provide some ways to avoid use of first person.

ways of saying

It could be suggested that ...

This is illustrated by ...

This/that is seen through ...

... is evident because ...

Close examination of the (visual image) enables ...

The evidence from the (visual image) includes ... and supports ...

This is exemplified by ...

... shows that ...

Therefore, it can be concluded that ...

In the (visual image) ... is apparent.

The creator of this (visual image) reveals ...

In the (visual image) ... is most obvious.

The (visual image) is most easily interpreted by ...

The inclusion of more detail/evidence/ information would help interpret this image.

When interpreting this (visual image) it is important to consider ...

The (visual image) evokes a feeling of ...

The main response to this (visual image) is one of ...

One use of the (visual image) could be to ...

A strong message is apparent in this (visual image) and this is ...

An alternative interpretation is ...

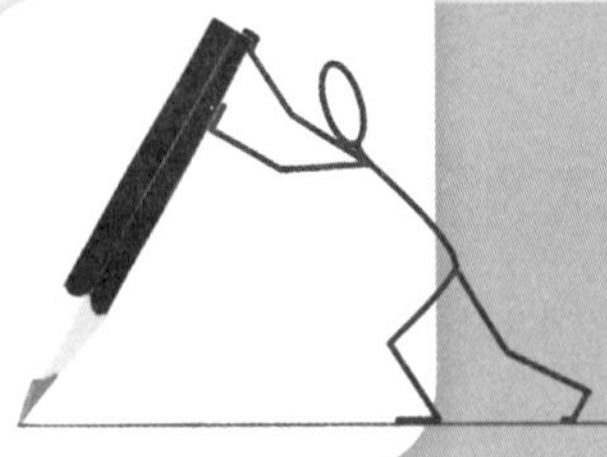

the vocabulary of visual images

angle/point of view	The angle of a camera shot that encourages the viewer to adopt a particular point of view. The degree of involvement and degree of power can be altered by changing the camera angle.
annotation	A note or comment added to a diagram that provides more information or explanation about the parts, or all of the image.
artistic/aesthetic elements	Aspects of an image that show beauty, placed in such a way to create an effective and innovative design.
ascending	Something that is ascending is moving towards a higher level or degree.
atmosphere/mood	A state of mind or feeling.
axis/axes	1. A real or imagined line(s) that goes through the centre of something (e.g. axis of symmetry). 2. (maths) The fixed reference line used in a graph to show the scale.
background	The part of the image that is the greatest distance from the viewer.
balance	A compositional technique that frames objects in equal weight.
brightness	The amount of light or contrast in an image.
blueprint	A scaled plan of a building or machinery, often printed in blue ink.
camera angle	The position of the camera in relation to the person or object being filmed or photographed. The angle is chosen to achieve certain effects.
caricature	A picture of a person in which certain characteristics are exaggerated to create a comic or grotesque effect.
cartoon	One or more simple drawings showing the features of people in a humorously exaggerated way, often for satirical or comic effect.
chart	1. A diagram or table that shows non-numeric information (words). 2. A map used for navigation by sea or air. 3. A sheet of paper or card, usually large, showing information in tabular or diagrammatic form.
compositional meaning	The ways in which objects are placed on a page – the layout.
declining/decreasing	Reducing or falling in number or quality.
demand	When participants in an image look directly in the viewer's eyes.
depiction	A life-like pictorial image of someone or something.
descending	Something that is descending is moving towards a lower level, amount or degree.
design	1. A decorative pattern or shape, sometimes repeated. 2. The plan for something, often used as a guide to its construction or manufacture.

the vocabulary of visual images

diagram	A drawing that shows the parts of something or how something works.
display	1. Information shown on a computer screen or similar device. 2. A collection of images for public viewing.
drawing	A pictorial image of someone or something, usually made using pencil, pen or crayon.
element	A characteristic or feature of an object such as form, line or shape.
extrapolate	1. To use known facts about something as a basis for a general statement about a situation, or suggesting what is likely to happen in the future. 2. (maths) To extend a graph to obtain additional values.
figure	1. A term used in publications for a visual image. 2. A diagram of a two- or three-dimensional geometric shape.
flowchart	A diagram of the sequence of steps involved in a complex system or procedure, for example a computer program.
foreground	The part of the image that is closest to the viewer.
framing	How boundaries make the viewer focus on a particular part of an image.
generic	A common feature or characteristic that can be said to be more general than specific.
graph	1. A pictorial device that shows numeric information, often compared with one or more axes. 2. A diagram of a network showing vertices (nodes) and edges (connecting lines).
graphic	A pictorial representation of something, often produced by computer.
hierarchy	An arrangement of things in order of importance, usually from least important to most important.
horizontal	Something that is parallel to the horizon, at right angles to the vertical.
icon or symbol	A symbol or simplified drawing used to represent an idea, thing or activity, often used in computing.
illumination	The effect that light has in an image and degrees of intensity of light.
illustration	A drawing, diagram or photograph of something that accompanies printed, spoken or electronic text.
image	1. A picture or likeness of someone or something. 2. A visible representation of someone or something produced by light reflecting in a mirror or passing through a lens, often onto a screen.
increasing	Something that is increasing is becoming greater in size, amount or degree.
infographic	A chart containing diagrams, symbols and text showing the different aspects of an idea, information or data.
information value	How the information on the page is valued – left vs right, up vs down.
inner	Situated farthest from the edge of an image.
interactive or interpersonal meaning	How images engage the viewer by the use of emotions.

interpolate
1. To insert something of a different nature into something else.
2. (maths) To use a graph to deduce an unknown value that lies between two known values.

key
An explanation of the symbols and numbers used in a visual image; more specific than a legend.

label
A word or phrase attached to an image to provide information to assist with interpreting the image.

legend
A caption or title added to an image to provide a brief explanation of the features of the image; more general than a key.

map
1. A diagrammatic representation of all or part of the earth's surface (usually).
2. A diagram showing the connections between ideas or between the elements of two sets.

meta-function
Like meta-language, meta-functions refer to how people discuss the meanings in images using various factors.

model
1. A three-dimensional representation of something, usually on a different scale than the original.
2. A systematic representation of an object or idea that shares important characteristics with the original.

musical score
The written or printed symbols arranged to represent vocal or instrumental sound.

network
A group of interconnected people or things.

offer
When a person in an image does not directly look at the viewer.

order
An arrangement of things in relation to each other according to a particular sequence, size, pattern or method.

outer
Situated closest to the periphery or edge of an image.

painting
A picture of someone or something prepared using paint.

participant
Any object, person or place featured in an image.

pattern
A repeating decorative design or shape.

perspective
The way that three-dimensional objects appear on two-dimensional surfaces to give an accurate impression of their height, width, depth and position in relation to each other.

photograph
An exact visual representation of someone or something produced by a camera.

picture
A painting, drawing, photograph or portrait of someone or something.

plan
A drawing or diagram of the layout or arrangement of something.

plot
A graph, map or diagram that marks the location or motion of something.

point of view
The position from which something or someone is observed. This can be influenced by camera angle and zooming in or out.

print
An exact reproduction of a picture, usually on paper.

relative (to)
Something that is relative to something else is compared with it.

representation or representational meaning
A picture, model, or other depiction of someone or something.

the vocabulary of visual images

salience The feature of an image that draws the most attention.

scale A method of showing the size or amount of something that can be measured. A scale can be shown in three ways:

1. It can be a system of marks set at fixed intervals (often on an axis) used as a standard for measurement.
2. Words can be used to indicate the relationship between the representation and what it represents (e.g. 1 cm represents 1 km).
3. It can be a mathematical ratio that compares the size of the representation and what it represents (e.g. 1:10 000).

scale drawing A representation of something with all dimensions reduced or increased in the same proportion.

semiotics The study of signs and symbols.

shape The form of an object.

sketch A drawing, picture or graph that is done quickly and roughly.

social distance The amount of space made between the viewer and the participants (e.g. close-up, mid or long distance).

superimpose To place or lay something (picture or words) over another thing so that both parts can be seen at the same time.

symmetry Something is symmetrical when one half is a mirror image of the other half. There can be several lines of symmetry.

tessellation An arrangement of shapes, often polygons, closely fitted together in a repeated pattern without gaps or overlapping.

texture The feel, appearance or consistency (roughness or smoothness) of a surface.

trend A general direction in which something is developing or changing.

typical A part of an image that is repeated in other parts of the image and which can be interpreted in the same way as the first part. A representation is typical of something when it shows the features commonly found in the original.

vector The line of sight when viewing an image (i.e. where the eye starts from and travels to).

vertical Something that lies at right angles to the horizontal plane so that the top is directly above the bottom.

visual aid An image or model of something that is used to assist understanding.

visual image A print or electronic picture or representation of something or someone.

visual representation A print or electronic picture or image of something or someone.

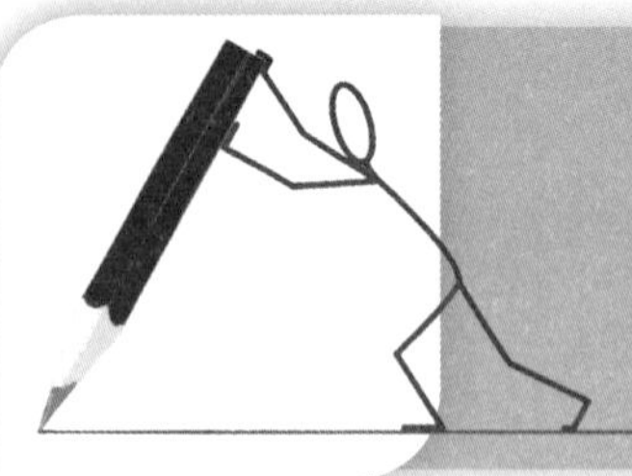

teacher information

Visual representations are a feature of modern life. They include diagrams, illustrations, photographs, artworks, scale drawings, maps, charts, figures, icons, graphs, plots, networks, sketches, animations, and plans. For the purposes of this book, a *visual image* is defined as a print or electronic picture or representation of something or someone. The term *visual images* is used in preference to other terms such as *graphics, information graphics*, or *graphical images* to avoid the suggestion that visual representations are limited to graphs, or confusion with the learning area in many secondary schools that is known as graphics. Visual images are commonly used to display information, both quantitative and qualitative, but they can also be used to enrich texts and appeal to the emotions.

Students are likely to encounter a wide variety of visual images, both at school and elsewhere. The extent of this variety makes it difficult for teachers to expose students to every possibility. It follows that an approach to writing about visual images that aims to teach students about every variation of each type of visual image is neither practical nor likely to be successful. The traditional approach to the teaching of visuals is by purpose, with little transfer of knowledge between contexts. For example, number lines, linear measuring scales, measuring gauges, and timelines all rely on the interpretation of a scale in a single dimension, but they are taught as discrete topics in different learning areas, implying that they differ from each other. However, it is the characteristics (properties) of a visual (e.g. scale, direction, shape, colour) that primarily determine how it is decoded. A teaching approach that focuses on the properties of visual images is more likely to assist students in making meaning and in transferring knowledge between visual images with similar properties.

There are four ways of reading texts:

- **Skimming** – involves glancing or browsing the text, similar to the way a reader might read a magazine. The reader wants to get a general idea of what is in the text. Not everything is read.
- **Scanning** – involves searching for something specific. The text is read with the purpose of locating key ideas or information. Scanning is more purposeful and deliberate than skimming.

- **Continuous** – involves reading (usually words) in a sustained way, similar to the way novels are read.
- **Close** – involves reading something in detail and looking closely at every feature of the text.

When reading visual images, scanning (looking for specifics) and close reading (paying attention to all the details) are more important reading practices than skimming and continuous reading.

Other information related to reading visual images has been shared by researchers such as Gunther Kress and Theo van Leeuwen. According to Kress and van Leeuwen (2006)[1], visual images can be analysed by referring to three different meanings:

- representational or ideational meaning
- interpersonal or interactive meaning
- compositional or textual meaning.

Representational meaning refers to the subject matter or what is often referred to as *field* in the linguistic mode. It is about who or what is involved in the image (the participants) as well as the circumstances or setting in which these occur.

Interpersonal meaning refers to the impact the image has on the viewer. It is also referred to as *tenor* for language, and is concerned with relationships between the characters in the text and also between the reader/viewer and the author/illustrator.

Compositional meaning or *mode* is about the layout, that is, where objects and people are placed on the page or screen. This includes the relative emphasis on particular elements and the distribution of these. For example, designers choose the colour, size and style of a font for particular purposes.

This book assists students to write in a variety of forms. These forms are arranged in the book from lower order to higher order, according to Bloom's Taxonomy.

1 Kress, G., & van Leeuwen, T. (2006). *Reading images: A grammar of visual design* (2 ed.). London: Routledge.

visual image credits

Sketch: pencil pusher (on many pages): Zsuzsanna Killan

describing (pages 6 to 11)

Example 1: Protractor: prepared by L Carter

Example 2: Electrical circuit: iStock.com/haryigit (stock illustration ID: 494755264)

Example 3: Rainforest: Reproduced with permission of Arkie Barton

Example 4: Photograph – Row of houses: iStock.com/swedewah (stock illustration ID: 589446116)

explaining (pages 12 to 17)

Example 1: Topographic map: iStock.com/judywatt (stock illustration ID: 172153240)

Example 2: Student exposure to words pie chart: prepared by L Carter

Example 3: Coke can and sugar: iStock.com/Bychykhin_Olexandr (stock illustration ID: 473307874)

Example 4: My Mother's Country: reproduced with permission of Robert Barton

inferring (pages 18 to 23)

Example 1: Global temperature change graph: prepared by L Carter

Example 2: Computer postures: Can Stock Photo Inc./W Mitchelle

Example 3: Cartoon – Woman hides the child: iStock.com/stegworkz (stock illustration ID: 509240468)

Example 4: Photograph – Man on ledge: iStock.com/Alija (stock illustration ID: 528920316)

interpreting (pages 24 to 29)

Example 1: Box-and-whisker plot: prepared by L Carter

Example 2: SE Queensland rail network: reproduced with permission from Queensland Rail

Example 3: Photograph – Women on bench: iStock.com/Anna Bryukhanova (stock illustration ID: 459003273)

Example 4: Cartoon – Hour glass: iStock.com/xochicalco (stock illustration ID: 505685466)

visual image credits

comparing: (pages 30 to 35)

Example 1: Chart – Fastest animals on land: prepared by L Carter

Example 2: Flowchart: prepared by L Carter

Example 3: Photograph – Red farmhouse: iStock.com/carroteater (stock illustration ID: 104882816)

Photograph – Haunted house: iStock.com/everlite (stock illustration ID: 506473896)

Example 4: Picture – 1950s domestic goddess: iStock.com/sturti (stock illustration ID: 143919742)

analysing (pages 36 to 41)

Example 1: Cricket wagon wheel: prepared by L Carter

Example 2: Water molecule: iStock.com/StasKhom (stock illustration ID: 175121136)

Example 3: Picture – Broken robot: iStock.com/piranka (stock illustration ID: 512989686)

Example 4: Cartoon – Outcast girl: iStock.com/yelet (stock illustration ID: 475249245)

critiquing: (pages 42 to 47)

Example 1: Conical graph: prepared by L Carter

Example 2: Illustration – Food pyramid: iStock.com/bilhagolan (stock illustration ID: 164021614)

Example 3: Sketch – Australian settlement: alamy stock photo GIDJFA

Example 4: Photo – Graffiti: iStock.com/kurga (stock illustration ID: 467921573)

reflecting (pages 48 to 53)

Example 1: Cigarette graph: prepared by L Carter

Example 2: Sound chart: prepared by L Carter, photograph of ear used with permission of Fraunhofer-Gesellschaft (http://hearcom.eu/lenya/hearcom/authoring/main/usertrials/02A12B8G.jpg)

Example 3: Photograph – Snapshots: iStock.com/IvanJekic (stock illustration ID: 539236041)

Example 4: Illustration – Seaside: iStock.com/smartboy10 (stock illustration ID: 507072080)

my useful words and phrases

my useful words and phrases

my useful words and phrases

my useful words and phrases

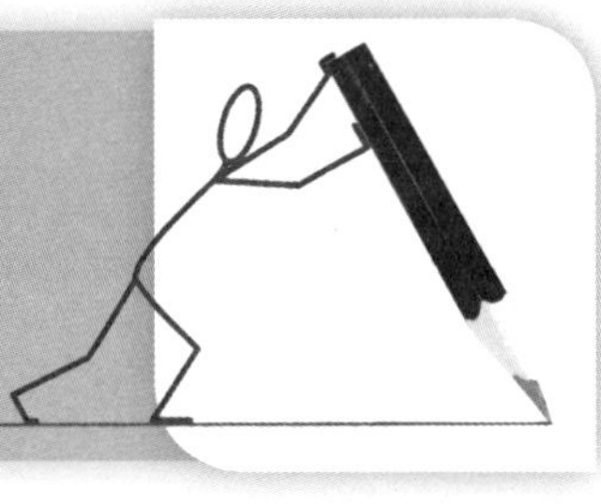

ISBN 9780987215901
Pages 56

How to write what you want to say … in the secondary years

Patricia Hipwell

This book will significantly improve writing skills for people who have to complete assignments, essays, reports and recommendations.

Students will improve their marks by using the easy to understand methods of answering questions set by examiners.

ISBN 9781925046038
Pages 64

How to write what you want to say … in mathematics

Lyn Carter and Patricia Hipwell

It is a common fallacy that mathematics doesn't require students to write. The writing demands of this subject are different from other subjects. This book provides students with language in the form of sentence starters, connectives and useful mathematical language to enable them to write correctly.

How to write what you want to say… in mathematics: a guide for students of mathematics who know what they want to say but can't find the words provides parents, teachers and students with a unique tool for improving mathematical writing. Suitable for students from the middle years of schooling to tertiary level.

ISBN 9781925046489
Pages 96

How to write what you want to say … in the primary years

Catherine Black and Patricia Hipwell

Young writers who struggle with putting their ideas into writing need language to help them. This book provides that language in the form of sentence starters and connectives. It also provides graphic organisers to help young writers organise their thoughts – a process necessary for good writing.

How to write what you want to say… in the primary years: a guide for primary students who know what they want to say but can't find the words provides parents, teachers and young writers with a tool for improving writing. It is suitable for Years 2 to 6.

ISBN	9781925236910
Pages	64

How to write what you want to say ... in business

Lyn Carter and Patricia Hipwell

This guide provides those in business and government with the language they need to write for a variety of purposes. It aims to provide those with limited experience in these forms of writing with a starting point to say what they want to say using language that mature writers use.

How to write what you want to say ... in business is a guide for those who know what they want to say but can't find the words. It provides a unique tool for improving writing. It seeks to assist inexperienced writers of business and government communications and also students of business courses from the middle years of schooling to the tertiary and vocational level.

ISBN	9781925236903
Pages	74

How to write what you want to say ... in science

Malcolm Carter, Lyn Carter and Patricia Hipwell

This guide provides students with the language they need to write for a variety of purposes in science. It aims to provide inexperienced writers with a starting point to say what they want to say using language that mature writers use.

How to write what you want to say ... in science is a guide for those who know what they want to say but can't find the words. It provides a unique tool for improving scientific writing. It suits inexperienced scientific writers from the middle years of schooling to tertiary level.

ISBN	9781925236927
Pages	84

How to write what you want to say ... at university

Patricia Hipwell and Lyn Carter

This guide provides students at university and other tertiary institutions with the language they need to write for scholarly, or academic, purposes. It aims to provide those with limited experience in academic writing with a starting point to say what they want to say using language that academic writers use.

How to write what you want to say ... at university is a guide for those who know what they want to say but can't find the words. It suits inexperienced writers enrolled in undergraduate courses at university, including those for whom English is a second language. It is especially helpful to mature-aged students returning to study.

about the authors

Patricia Hipwell M.Ed., B.Sc. Econ. (Hons), Grad. Dip. of Literacy Ed., P.G.C.E., is an independent literacy consultant for her own company, **logonliteracy**. She delivers literacy professional development to teachers in Australia, and works predominantly in Queensland schools. Patricia has specialised in assisting all teachers to be literacy teachers, especially high school subject specialists who often struggle with what it means to be a content area teacher and a literacy teacher.

Merilyn (Lyn) Carter Ph.D., M.Ed. (Research), Dip.Ed., B.Ec., is also an independent consultant with **Count on Numeracy and a researcher at the Queensland University of Technology**, specialising in numeracy and mathematics education. Her doctoral thesis investigated NAPLAN numeracy testing.

Georgina Barton Ph.D., B.A., Dip. Teach., Grad. Cert. Higher Ed., is an Associate Professor in the School of Teacher Education and Early Childhood at the University of Southern Queensland. She teaches literacy and English education courses in the tertiary context and has been a teacher in schools for over 20 years. She is the President of Meanjin local council for the Australian Literacy Educators Association and regularly works with teachers and students in schools.

Patricia and Lyn have created many resources to assist students' literacy and numeracy development. Patricia, Lyn and Georgina are available (as a cross-curricular team or individually) to provide professional development in their areas of expertise and to support the use of their recommended resources, including this one.

The authors acknowledge the assistance of Malcolm Carter for writing the science and cricket examples, Rob Barton for allowing the reproduction of his artwork on page 17, and Charlotte Cottier AE for editing.

For further information, contact:

Patricia Hipwell, 0429 727 313, pat.hipwell@gmail.com

Merilyn (Lyn) Carter, 0402 077 958, countonnumeracy@bigpond.com

Georgina Barton, 0421 169 039, Georgina.Barton@usq.edu.au